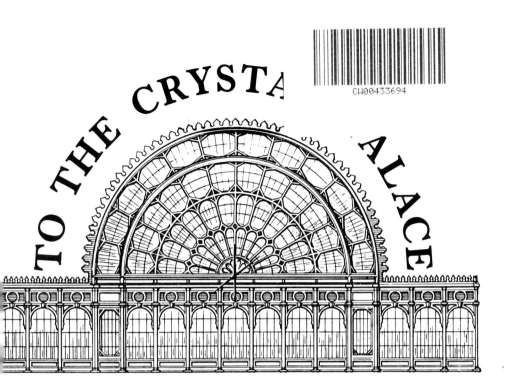

CRYSTAL

TO THE

PALACE

CW00433694

C.T. GOODE

Forge Books

Published by Forge Books
55 Brookside, Wokingham
Berks RG11 2ST

ISBN 904662-13-6

First published 1984
Reprinted 1993

© C. T. Goode

Printed by Short Run Press, Ltd, Exeter

Contents

Chapter 1. 'The fine Crystal Palace the Prince had built'.   7
Chapter 2. A new Home in South London   11
Chapter 3. Making Tracks to the People's Palace   15
Chapter 4. A High Level Approach   19
Chapter 5. Days of Delight   23
Chapter 6. Halcyon Days   29
Chapter 7. Electrification on the Grand Scale   31
Chapter 8. Wartime and Thereafter   35
Chapter 9. The Great Conflagration   39
Chapter 10. The Long Hiatus   43

Appendix 1. The Crystal Palace and the Early Years of Association
            Football by the Rev. Nigel Sands, Historian to
            Crystal Palace Football Club   49
Appendix 2. Trams and Trolley Buses   52
Appendix 3. Time Tables   54

from Child's Book facsimile
— The Fine Crystal Palace the Prince Had Built

Published by Dean & Son in their 'Aunt Busy Bee's' series, published 1851–2

Introduction

The Author makes no excuse for the appearance of this little work, other than that it is to be regarded as a companion to his earlier work on a similar edifice built in the north on Muswell Hill, that copy called Alexandra Palace. It was only after completing that and researching various references that he found that, surprisingly, though quite a lot had been written about the Palace as a building and popular resort, not a great amount had appeared on the stations which served it, both fine structures in themselves and worthy of more than just a passing glance.

Today anyone possessed of a vivid imagination can go to the top of Westow Hill and try to fix the location of that gigantic greenhouse, the tram shelters and facade of the High Level station. All he (or she) will have to go on will be a flattened site for the Palace and an oblong hole with a fragment of retaining wall for the upper station. By the road on the hill is the round foundation for the south tower. At Low Level the atmosphere is still there in a section of upper concourse with draughty arches and steps. The push and pull steam working would certainly have raised the echoes here!

I have drawn on the notes made by Mr. R.C. Riley and others in past issues of railway publications, and am indebted to the Librarians at West Norwood, Bromley, Croydon and at the new GLC Record Office for their assistance and patience. Mr. Casserley has again turned up trumps with very relevant material. The special contribution by the Rev Nigel Sands is a fascinating addition to the story.

C. Tony Goode.
Anlaby, Hull.

Bibliography

'Paxton's Palace'. Bird. Cassell.
'History of the London, Brighton & South Coast Railway.' Turner. Batsford.
'Southern Electric.' Moody. Ian Allan.
'Crystal Palace.' Beaver. Hugh Evelyn.

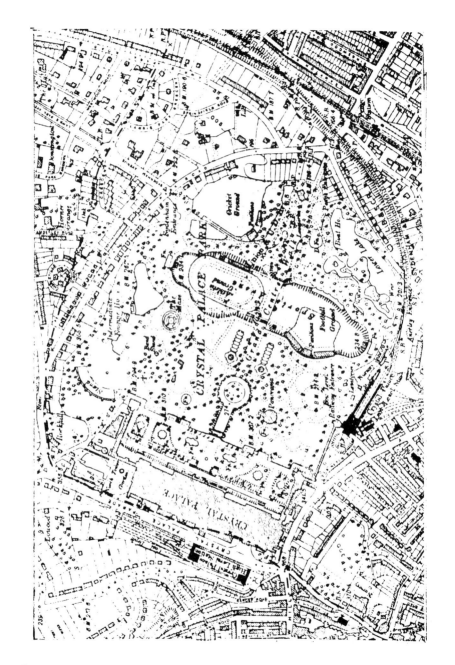

1

'The Fine Crystal Palace The Prince Had Built'

Several splendid books have been written on the Great Exhibition of 1851 with its vast display of resources and inventiveness culled from the Empire and indeed all parts of the world. It is however wise to set out the general development of schemes and to record the important features in the history of one of the most well-known and spectacular structures in the world, which drew millions of people to it, most making use of the railway during each year of its existence, especially when at Sydenham.

Fairs to display and promote industrial and artistic enterprise had been held regularly for many years before 1851. They were popular in Germany and France, particularly Leipzig and Paris, and the first Society of Arts Fair was held in this country in 1756. 'Arts' meant any sort of inventive skill and often produced some hideous mixtures of the mechanical and biological calculated to produce the vapours in Victorian ladies. There were fairs in Dublin from 1829, while a Bazaar of British Manufacturers was held at Convent Garden in 1845. The engineer Robert Stephenson persuaded the Society of Arts to set up an Exhibition of Products of National Industry which was unfortunately unable to invoke the right support.

It was due to the interest shown by three gentlemen that the Great Exhibition was finally launched. Prince Albert, Queen Victoria's Consort from Thuringia, was well known for his interest in worldly material progress and would give the Royal cachet. More practically, Henry Cole was in a position of authority at the Public Record Office, a forceful man who had many strings to his bow, being the editor of 'The Journal of Design' wherein efforts were constantly made to encourage designers to improve everyday artefacts. Cole was interested in experiments in reproducing illustrations by electro-typography and, it is said, produced the very first Christmas card in 1846. He produced illustrated books for children and, in a different direction, set his talents to work on a British bone china tea service, produced by Minton. Here were two men, full of ideas and ambition. Prince Albert was most probably glad of an excellent excuse to free himself somewhat of the restrictions of royalty. He became President of the Society of Arts in 1846, and as a consequence it acquired the prefix 'Royal'. Exhibitions were held at

7

intervals, for which the groundwork was carried out by Henry Cole who canvassed factories up and down the country for ideas.

In 1849 a Grand Exposition was held in Paris, fitted in during a convenient lull between revolutions. This was successful and planted the germ of the idea for a Great Exhibition, originally destined for the courtyard of Somerset House, an idea scotched by Albert who proposed instead a site in Hyde Park, near the Barracks. Given the identity of the proposer, royal assent was given for Hyde Park to be used from February 1850 and a Committee was formed to deal with the various matters of building, financial disposal and exhibits. Prince Albert presided over a worthy body of thirty members, including Lord Granville, Sir Robert Peel, William Gladstone, Mr. Cubitt (the builder) and Mr. Barry (the architect).

The Royal Commission was willing to consider ideas from any quarter for the design of a suitable building to house the Exhibition and these, some 245 in all, came in from many parts of the world. The contribution by Brunel was a disappointment, an unpleasant-looking monster with a 50ft. dome some 200ft. in diameter.

At this point the third member of the triumvirate, Joseph Paxton, enters the story. Paxton was a gardener working in the grounds of the Royal Horticultural Society which happened to be next to the Duke of Devonshire's estates at Chiswick. His work impressed the Duke to such an extent that he invited Paxton to work on his lands at Chatsworth House. Here he was most successful and displayed his ingenuity to the full, not only with plants but also with his fountains and other devices; the jet of water from his largest creation reached up to 267ft. Greenhouses and conservatories went up apace and a large imported water lily (called Victoria) had its own glass cover held aloft by delicate iron tracery like leaf veins, hollow to collect the rain water.

From now on Joseph Paxton's future was assured. He literally moved a whole village from the Park gates to afford a better view from the House, took charge of the running of the Duke's estates, went abroad with him and found time to write books, edit a newspaper and sit on the Board of Directors of the Midland Railway. It was due to this office that Paxton met Henry Cole through the agency of the chairman of the MR, and as the acquaintanceship developed, so did Paxton's interest in producing a large structure which would be easy and swift to assemble to cover the proposed exhibition and just as simple to dismantle after use. Already the ambitious gardener had stage-managed a display for Queen Victoria at Chatsworth in 1843 with lighting and water effects all of which was cleared away by the following day. Here then was a master of quickly assembled spectacles who promised that he would design his Great Exhibition building in nine days; in fact, with the assistance of Barlow the MR Engineer, Paxton managed it in seven, working in the Chatsworth estate office. The design was very much a huge greenhouse in aspect, built to what would be called nowadays 'modular' patterns with the ruling size of each section 24ft. divisible by 3. The whole structure was up in Hyde Park in 22 weeks from its commencement on 22nd. September 1850, and the interior fitting and painting took a further sixteen weeks. The actual building was carried out by Fox & Henderson, while the all-important glass, some 18 acres of it, was supplied by Chance Bros. of Birmingham.

Three large elm trees on the site were accommodated in a manner which would please conservationists today, by having the roof arch constructed high enough to let them grow on happily inside. This caused the symmetry of the roof profile to be out by some 48ft. and gave ruling heights of 63ft. for the nave and 198ft. for the large transept. The total cost of the building was about £200,000 and it was open for the reception of goods on 12th. February 1851.

There was opposition to the idea of siting such a huge building in a popular London resort, chiefly on the grounds of appearance, that a temporary building could easily linger and that such a 'Crystal Palace', Punch's sobriquet for it, would attract scum and foreigners. However, Queen Victoria opened the Exhibition on 1st. May 1851 and it was to continue in full swing for a further 141 days except Sundays, with the initial three guinea seasons for men, two guineas for women, subsequently reduced to 30/- and £1 respectively. The day rate of admission was reduced by degrees from £1 to 1/-, and by the end just over six million people had attended, very many of them coming just to see the Palace itself. There was no smoking allowed, and no alcoholic drinks were sold, only sherbet and tea as accompaniments to light refreshments especially bath buns of which one million were consumed. The closing ceremony on 15th. October 1851 was attended by about 50,000, not the greatest number however as 110,000 had paid admission eight days before, Profits were of the order of £186,437, while Messrs. Paxton, Fox and Cubitt received knighthoods, Henry Cole getting a CBE.

There was of course no direct link with Hyde Park by rail, but most of the railway companies offered a generous 2/6d rail ticket which was available from any station and included admission for any day while the Exhibition was being held.

> As though 'twere by a wizard's rod
> A blazing arch of lucid glass
> Leaps like a fountain from the grass
> To meet the sun!

Crystal Palace with lower terrace retaining wall in foreground @ 1860

Crystal Palace in 1900 from the Parade

2

A New Home in South London

For several months after all was over, the Palace stood empty while its future was debated. Paxton was, perhaps, reluctant to put his powers of quick dismantling to the test and suggested that it stay in situ as a leisure complex. His early reputation had been somewhat tarnished by suggestions that credit for the idea of an iron and glass structure used as an exhibition house and winter garden should have gone to William Bridges Adams who had, in fact published an article on the subject some three months before Paxton. However, the job was done and the next task was to secure the Palace's future. On 30th. April 1852 Parliament decided that the elms could come out of hiding and that the structure should be moved. As from 18th. May 1852 the Crystal Palace Company Ltd. was formed to purchase the building with £500,000 capital in £5 shares. The purchase price was a mere £75,000 and the cost of transport and re-erection which Fox & Henderson were to undertake was £120,000.

What was at the time the largest clock in the world dominated the Exhibition, but on removal it was decided that the mechanism was not required and so it was purchased by the Great Northern Railway for King's Cross station. Bells inscribed with the names of Queen and Consort were also supplied and fitted as part of the works on the roofing behind the tower and it is believed that they were in use up to the outbreak of the Great War.

At this juncture the railway interest comes into play for Samuel Laing, the Chairman and, a majority shareholder of the new Crystal Palace Company was also Chairman of the London, Brighton and South Coast Railway Company.

Efforts were made to establish that the new Palace was indeed new; more splendid and worthy than the original. When on 5th August 1852 the work was inaugurated by the erection of a first pillar brought from Hyde Park, Mr Laing in his address was moved to an ecstasy of religious and uplifting sentiments: "Figure to yourselves the surrounding area . . . converted into a crystal dome and raised aloft under the blue canopy of heaven, and you will form some indistinct image of the new central transept (which) will shortly exist as a tangible reality for the wonder and admiration of millions"

11

Opportunity was taken to make some alterations to the design of the Palace, especially as there were no elm trees to incorporate, so that the large transept was in fact raised, two smaller transepts were added to increase width and a semi-circular roof appeared along the total length, the whole structure now being six storeys high instead of three, with three transepts instead of one. The new venture incidentally never made a profit and went bankrupt, due to insufficient backing.

Another director of the LB & SCR, Leo Schulster, sold his 300 acre estate on the top of Sydenham Hill to the Crystal Palace Company, a site no more than one mile west of the main line from London Bridge overlooking it and vast areas of Kent. Here were comfortable villas to the north and west, while to the south and east everything was largely unspoilt. The suburban delights of Anerley, Penge and Sydenham were to develop in the years after the Palace had become established.

Fox & Henderson would no doubt have dearly liked a railway to move the components of the huge Meccano set, an apt comparison as all the parts did unbolt easily into their modules ready for transfer. From old site to new as the crow flies was twelve miles; actual was nearer twenty miles by horse and wagon across the Thames and through teeming South London to the foot of Sydenham Hill. Here the 1 in 8 slope was conquered by using extra teams of horses and traction engines. (Dealing with the glass was quite easy, for it was simply smashed, swept up and returned to Chance Bros. to be remade.) Protests came from the Animal Protection Society which raised its cudgels on behalf of the horses, working on a terrain which was not easy and level at Sydenham as it had been in Hyde Park, but falling to the east and needing a part basement.

A vast army of navvies, chiefly men weaned on railway building, arrived at Sydenham for the great work of construction. Their behaviour was usually disciplined and exemplary, although a chapter of misunderstandings led to a bloody 'Battle of Penge' with the police. Their presence coincided with the outbreak of the Crimean War, and the government turned to Paxton for help in the formation of an Army Works Corps of labourers for overseas service. The Palace became a main base for the Corps prior to embarkation.

A curious record of these days is "English Hearts and English Hands, or The Railway and the Trenches" written by a middle-class well-wisher, Catherine Marsh. One is torn between admiration for the courage and charity of the author and horror at the lofty condescension of some of the sentiments expressed: towards "that great mass who eat their bread under the heavier portion of the primeval curse".

Another innovation intended to cope with part of the work-force employed on the construction work was the first 'New Town! The rows of small terraced houses on the south side of Central Hill were surrounded by a wall, intended less to exclude intruders than to protect existing local residents from the more uncouth behaviour expected from the inhabitants of this ghetto. Paxton lived north of the site at a villa called 'Rockhills' from where he could keep an eye on affairs until his death in 1865. His vista included the new gardens which were a Victorian delight with walks, a maze, bandstands, terraces, replica prehistoric monsters and a set of fountains and cascades which called for 120,000 gallons of water every minute. This in turn called for the expertise of Brunel who designed twin towers to be sited on special cement foundations, one each side of the Palace, really large chimneys which were 284ft. high containing water tanks each to hold 300,000 gallons and with attendant pumps below.

Construction of the main building and towers began on 5th. August 1852, and the reopening took place on 10th. June 1854. The original estimates for completion had increased fourfold. There was a concert hall seating 4,000 and a huge organ to entertain them all. Outside, regular firework displays were held while the hungry could go in search of dinner in one of the east facing restaurants, for which the charge was anything from five shillings to four guineas, that is, if one were a first class visitor. A normal second class meal would cost twenty pence, while the rough and tumble could summon up something with beer for tenpence.

In the first thirty years the Palace was very popular and was the most visited attraction in London, this in spite of inability to open on Sundays when many more would have been likely to come. The extra revenue would have been most welcome and would probably have ensured the rebuilding of the North Transept which was destroyed by fire in 1866 and subsequently abandoned.

Although the entertainment was much to the fore, the Victorian precept of improving the mind was in evidence here with a fine collection of exotic plants and with a general theme of active mankind throughout different periods of history all over the world. There were Greek, Roman and Moorish tableaux to edify and uplift. In the grounds the monsters were hollow and could be entered, all in the cause of entertainment. In many respects Crystal Palace was ahead of its time with its conception of an unusual and active museum and the profits from the Great Exhibition and from the sale of the Palace were used to buy 87 acres of land at South Kensington, of which 40 acres were put to use as museum sites providing lasting pleasure and benefit. Much of this work was completed after Albert's death in 1862, and the Royal Albert Hall is his fitting memorial.

The Great Northern Railway had derived great financial benefits from running excursion traffic from the suburbs to the Great Exhibition. They liked what they saw happening at Sydenham and decided to sponsor a similar venture called Alexandra Palace on Muswell Hill, opened in 1862.

CRYSTAL PALACE.

200th ANNIVERSARY
— OF THE —
GRENADIER GUARDS.

WEDNESDAY, 25 JULY.

IN THE CENTRAL TRANSEPT.

MILITARY SPORTS & ATHLETIC GAMES.
MILITARY BANDS. AND CRYSTAL PALACE BAND, & GREAT ORGAN.
BALLOON ASCENT BY MR. COXWELL.
DISPLAY OF FOUNTAINS.
MAGNIFICENT SHOW OF ROSES IN THE ROSARY, &c.

ADMISSION, - ONE SHILLING.

SATURDAY, 28 JULY.

VOCAL AND INSTRUMENTAL
CONCERT AND FLORAL PROMENADE,
IN WHICH THE CELEBRATED
MADLLE. ARTÔT
And MR. SANTLEY will sing. with other Vocal & Instrumental Talent.

Admission 2s. 6d.   Reserved Seats 2s. 6d.

JONES AND CO., PRINTERS, CURSITOR STREET.)   (July 22d 1860. No. 752.

3

Making Tracks to the People's Palace

An Act authorising the Crystal Palace branch line was passed on 8th. July 1853, whereby the LB & SCR could take off a flying junction from the outside or Slow Croydon lines of the London Bridge to Croydon main line at Sydenham. To accommodate the works some slight deviation had to take place, while Sydenham station found itself with staggered platforms, a new up platform being provided south of the overbridge. The line was a short one of one mile five chains, rising at 1 in 63 for half a mile, curving west and then moderating to 1 in 340 to enter the Crystal Palace station area. Here a substantial station was provided, with four roads entering the site, the outer ones running up along the retaining walls and with three double faced island platforms between the lines to give the two centre roads a face on each side for quick alighting and entraining. A third retaining wall ran down the centre of the station, dividing the middle island platform. At the outer end of the station was a handily placed central turntable, while outside the roof to the south were a couple of carriage sidings. The roofing was arched in two bays with clerestory tops. Fourteen acres of land was purchased for the station, while the estimate for all the works was £85,000. The line was brought into use for freight on 27th. March 1854 and to passengers on 10th. June 1854. From the start some 10,000 passengers were carried each weekday.

The actual station building here was an imposing affair built high in grand manner, but not quite able to reflect the impressiveness of the mammoth structure it served; indeed, how could it? Within, the 72 foot span roof was supported by many wooden arches, the whole assembly calculated to strike awe and even fear into the uninitiated, scrambling up the imposing flights of stairs from the trains. From these premises it was possible to pass along a glass covered walkway of some 200 yards to the Palace direct, lined with creeping plants and tasteful if often nude statuary, a miniature elongated foretaste of the Palace itself. If one found, however, that the young female members of the family party were perhaps embarrassed by the explicit displays of the statuary or fearful of the creeping flora, then one could withdraw gracefully through handy gaps to the Lower or Upper Terraces.

The station at Crystal Palace was not to remain a terminus for very long, as

R.C. RILEY

32543 on Ramblers' Special to Chesham leaving Low Level 3rd June 1952

by an Act of 4th. August 1853 the West End of London & Crystal Palace Railway was to put down a line from Wandsworth to Crystal Palace, and beyond to Norwood Junction. Lines were extended through the back wall of the station from the second and fifth roads and out into a short stretch of open air beyond the Station Road bridge. From here a descent was made through a tunnel 745yd. long, followed by a second tunnel of 443yd. some two miles further on.

The first station was Gipsy Hill at $\frac{3}{4}$ mile from Crystal Palace on a falling gradient of 1 in 103 which stiffened to 1 in 83 and 1 in 69 for a spell. Some 74 chains beyond was Lower Norwood station, later West Norwood, again on a steep gradient and this time with curves to contend with as well. After this point the line rose through Leigham Court tunnel to Streatham, later Streatham Hill, a little over one mile from West Norwood. Thereafter the route took a more or less straight and uneventful course through Balham Hill Station to reach Wandsworth Common station $1\frac{1}{2}$ miles further on.

The line was opened on 1st. December 1856 and was considered as a westward extension of the Sydenham branch, so that down trains would arrive at Wandsworth from the east. The ultimate destination of the line was down by the Thames at Battersea Wharf, opened to regular traffic on 29th March 1858. The River Thames was crossed by the first trains on 1st. October 1860 when the Victoria Station & Pimlico Railway was opened, this coming into being through an Act of Parliament of 23rd. July 1858. Due to the height needed to clear river traffic, the construction of this small and vital section of line was difficult, and creating a headache in the form of a stiff gradient out of Victoria station, itself constructed on the flat.

The extension from Crystal Palace to Norwood Junction ran from the tunnel mouth in the open air well west of the station, skirting the enclosed platforms to the south and having two independent ones of its own. There were successive falling gradients at 1 in 81,1 in 106 and 1 in 95 to a flying connection at Norwood Jc.. This short stretch of line was opened on 1st. October 1857, and the engineers for both sections were Bidder, Fulton & Phipps. The contractors were Brassey, Peto & Betts.

To take the extension business a little further, a line was taken off the down line from Crystal Palace as it crossed the Croydon line near Norwood Junction, to run further east to Beckenham and Shortlands. This was part of an Act of 1854 which had envisaged a line to Farnborough in Kent. This section was taken over by the London, Chatham & Dover Railway as their own and a further extension was added from Shortlands to Southborough Road on 5th. July 1858. The West End & Crystal Palace lines were leased by the LB & SC from 1858, and were purchased in 1860.

Since the opening of the Palace several important suburban lines had been set up in quite short time, and more was to come. A glance at the map would show that potentially there were now facilities to be able to run trains between Victoria, Croydon and London Bridge. In practice, however, this was not feasible, due to the rather tortuous nature of the line and its fierce gradient profile. Instead, the easier, direct route through Thornton Heath was opened on 1st. December 1862, between East Croydon and Balham Hill.

With the development of the branch as a through route improvements were put in hand to relieve congestion and liven things up generally. The first alteration was the provision of steel arches instead of the earlier wooden ones supporting the roofing. Originally the landing at the top of the stairs was crudely equipped, dark and draughty, an inhospitable place to queue before passing through the turnstiles. In 1877, therefore, it was decided to spend £13,000 and build something more impressive, first widening the original road bridge by some ten feet to the rear, strengthening the area with wrought and cast iron girders with jack arches of nine inch brickwork between, levelled up with concrete. On this raft was placed a building in three sections, designed by Frederick Dale Banister and Whitney Mannering. The centre section contained a booking office and general waiting room 69ft. by 35ft. with a floor paved in Minton tiles. This was covered by a semi-circular oblong roof with a clerestory 12ft. wide and 4ft. high along the crest. The whole was originally stated to be a 'very handsome domed roof with cast iron principals and ornamental spandrels.' This structure was flanked by two other buildings; the one nearer the Palace had a very high pitched mansard roof covered in zinc and topped by an ornamental rail round the crowning square. The two storey building contained two corridors, each 41ft. by 11ft., 1st. and 2nd. Class Ladies' waiting rooms with lavatories, each 23ft by 15ft. and 18ft. by 17ft. respectively. On the site of the original buffet a larger dining room was provided with an adjacent refreshment bar. Alongside one of the corridors a large cloakroom 20ft. by 15ft. was provided. On the first floor a second dining room of 28ft. by 17ft. was to be found, together with kitchens. The structure on the south side was of more humble appearance with a domestic slate roof. On the ground floor this had the booking office, telegraph office and waiting rooms, the first and second class being fitted with carpets, chairs and tables, the third class more spartan in character. There were, however, plenty of lavatories. On the first floor were the station master's quarters which sported a living room, four bedrooms and a kitchen plus lavatory.

The carriageway in front of the station terminated in a space 70ft. by 40ft. covered by five bays, the portico glazed from ridges to gutters and resting on delicate iron columns with scrollwork. The construction was carried out by White of Croydon. Seen from the front, therefore, the station buildings were in effect three dissimilar ones, the one on the left which catered for the more affluent being the most impressive.

18

4

A High Level Approach

Another contender for the Crystal Palace traffic was the London, Chatham & Dover Company (the London, Smashem & Turnover as it was affectionately known) who, it will be remembered, had reached no further than Norwood Junction. They had opened their line from the Medway as far as Bickley in December 1860 and had been allowed to run into Victoria via the new route through Crystal Palace between 1860 and 1863, until their new route via Sydenham Hill was completed in July of that year. They were not, however, allowed to steal any LB & SC traffic between Victoria and Crystal Palace in either direction! A line from Herne Hill to Ludgate Hill was opened in 1864, extended to a junction with the Metropolitan at Farringdon Street in 1866 and reaching the terminus at Holborn Viaduct much later in 1874.

By an Act of 17th. July 1862 their Crystal Palace & South London Railway was to run from the City line at Brixton through Peckham Rye via Nunhead up to Crystal Palace, serving an independent station there at a higher level than that of the LB & SCR. At the same time the LB & SCR were promoting a South London line connecting its West End terminus at Victoria with its City terminus at London Bridge. This line duplicated the path of the Crystal Palace line between Peckham Rye and Brixton, and so it was decided by the Brighton Company to construct a four track section here, with the northern pair of lines to be used by LC & DR trains. As a reciprocal gesture the latter company constructed four tracks between Brixton and Battersea and allowed the rival company the use of two of them.

Stations on the branch were at Honor Oak, Lordship Lane and Upper Sydenham, and there were two tunnels, the one near Crystal Palace being 439yd. long and named after Paxton whose large house stood above it. The terminus was situated soon after the tunnel exit, placed in cutting so that excited families would find that they had crept up on the Palace unawares. The ruling gradient on the branch was 1 in 70. For the Low Level passengers arriving from Sydenham there would be superb views over the Park and dinosaurs to the Palace on its hill, up which they would then have to climb. The High Level passengers were simply directed to a columned and tiled underpass beneath the Parade and could be inside the great building within

19

minutes. Certainly this second site running from north to south and just across the road from the Palace's western facade was in a fine position. The new station here, called Crystal Palace and Upper Norwood was designed by Edward Barry and constructed for £100,000. Four lines entered the station which was covered by a rounded two bay roof similar to that at Low Level and resting, as there, on two side curtain walls and a central one, these in the form of rows of arches, the exterior ones filled and glazed in the upper parts. The outer lines ran up by each outside curtain wall, while the spaces between were filled by platforms, rather strangely made up of wooden boarding which was to prove unfortunate in the later stages of the station's history when rot set in, portions gave way and when ferny vegetation appeared in places to enhance the effect of an Edwardian conservatory. Outside, the ends of the building were matching, with the portion facing the roadway at the south end having a single storey building containing a central Classical portico flanked by three windows on each side of it. At each corner were square three storey towers, both with French turrets at each corner capped with ornamental railing. The same ideas were repeated at the inner end of the station facing arrivals. Here the four lines went through square openings in the walls which had sham arches above them at first floor level, while at second floor level were similar towers to those at the other end, together with the turrets.

Inside the station were two circulating areas on bridges above the centre lines at each end, with duplicated booking offices and refreshment rooms. The track layout here was of the neatest, no doubt suitably constrained by the limited site. There were seven carriage sidings parallel to each other on the departure side. One interesting feature was an extension of all four roads out into an air well beyond the road bridge to run to a turntable of 44ft. 10 in. diameter, which served the dual purpose of turning and releasing the train engines. The line was opened on 1st. August 1865 with a service between Victoria and Crystal Palace. Trains to the City were to be instituted later on, after the spur round to Loughborough Junction had been put in.

By an Act of 17th. July 1862 the South London Junction Company proposed an extension of the High Level branch south west to South Norwood, then east to Bromley Junction and over the spur to the Beckenham area but this was not proceeded with. There was also an associated proposal, also a non-starter, for a branch off the above running north west to connect with the West End & Crystal Palace line at Lower Norwood and Streatham Hill (Streatham & Brixton Hill). Not to be outdone, and seeing the handy location of the rival station compared with their own, the LB & SCR in 1859 sought unsuccessfully a short extension to run from Low Level into the Palace grounds and up to the north east corner of the site by the Upper Terrace.

Victorian grandeur. The exterior of the High Level Station

LENS OF SUTTON

Farewell rail tour at High Level – 19th Sept. 1954

21

R.C. RILEY
In 1954 Low Level shows its age and signs of neglect

R.C. RILEY
Battersea to Norwood goods hauled by 31914 passing Low Level 12th March 1954

22

5

Days of Delight

The Palace was a safe haven of industry and entertainment for all the family, for it was fire proof with many exits clearly marked and with a nine inch main serving twenty five fire points. The preoccupation with fire was possibly to result in the ultimate temptation of Providence many years later-or was it Providence? On the night that the North Transept was consumed by flames, on 30th. December 1866 the Rev. H.M. Hart was due to give a lecture on 'Fire; what causes it and how it is extinguished'. One wonders what he felt subsequently, and whether his credentials were checked! The heating was by hot water radiators and, unlike the situation in Hyde Park, cooking of hot meals was carried out on gas and coal ranges. It is not clear as to whether the no smoking rule was relaxed. The diversions available were many, and most planned events included displays of Brock's fireworks! For a time a 600yd. pneumatic railway linked the Sydenham and Penge entrances. This was the brain child of Mr. T.W. Rammell, an experimental affair on which passengers could travel in the afternoons for sixpence. The line ran in a ten foot tunnel and sported a gradient of 1 in 15 and a sharp curve along its length. There was one coach running on the broad gauge, fitted with sliding doors at each end and with seats for 85 passengers. The principle of operation was the same as that of the bicycle pump, whereby a diaphragm closed up against the sides of the cylinder and was blown or drawn according to direction. In the case of the coach a diaphragm encircled it and more or less sealed it off. Gravity and momentum both played a part in the exercise, helped by steam which powered the 22ft. diameter fan. The journey must have been an eery one and one hopes that some sort of lighting was provided. Probably the line lasted no longer than a year or two; however, it did stimulate similar experiments in London and Liverpool, the former failing through lack of cash, the latter under the Mersey eventually settling for conventional steam power. A gas operated Zoetrope (a kind of large what-the-butler-saw) was installed in 1868, while the Great Aquarium was opened in 1872. The usual admission charge was a shilling which admitted a visitor to all the spectacles and permanent exhibits, and in the first thirty years up to two million attended each year, most travelling by the trains which were ample, though sometimes lacking in first class compartments. A contemporary diary entry of 1862 makes a telling point:

'Yesterday we went, according to annual custom, to the Dramatic Fete at the Crystal Palace. I had four ladies to take charge of, and managed the difficult operation satisfactorily. I am no judge of numbers, but estimated the visitors at about 25,000. The Railway Company were much to blame for the utterly insufficient supply of first class carriages. The admission at the Palace being 2s. 6d., of course very few, if any, of the passengers took second class tickets and none third class, yet the second and third class carriages exceeded the first class in number and we, having taken first class returns, went to the Palace in a third class, open at the sides-sheep truck is a more appropriate name for it, and returned in a third class carriage'.

From those early days come two illustrations of what was on offer for those who, having endured a 'sheep truck' and run the gauntlet of the statuary, entered the portals.

'Mr. F. Strange, Contractor for the Supply of Refreshments, will hold his first fete on Wednesday, 28th. September when the undermentioned Entertainments will be provided.

An English Concert, supported by upwards of Eighty Vocalists under the Direction of Mr. P. Corri.
Mr. E.W. Mackney will sing several of his most popular Songs etc.
Under the direction of Mr. C. Godfrey the Band of the Coldstream Guards will perform some of the pieces in their repertoire.
The most celebrate Juvenile Musicians of Europe, The Cremona Band will appear for the first time in their popular Entertainment.
Performance on the Handel Festival Organ by Mr. James Coward.
Aquatic Sports on the Tidal Lakes. Boat racing for Prizes.
Paired oared match for two Silver Cups. Scullers' Match for money Prizes.
Walking the Horizontal Pole over the Lake. Wash Tub Race. Duck Hunt.
For the first time at the Palace there will be an ascent of a Monster Balloon from the Great Walk in the Park.
In the course of the Afternoon there will be a Display of the whole series of Great Fountains, including the Cascades, Dancing Fountains, Waterfalls, Pyramids, Basket Fountains and the Monster Jets upwards of Two Hundred and Fifty Feet high.
Admission One Shilling. Refreshments at the Usual Prices.'

'200th Anniversary of the Grenadier Guards. Wednesday, 25th. July 1860.
Great Dinner of 2,000 Men in the Central Transept.
Military Sports and Athletic Games. Balloon Ascent by Mr. Coxwell.
Magnificent Show of Roses in the Rosary. Admission One Shilling.'

24

Fetes and Exhibitions were likely to be held at any time for every conceivable reason, usually bringing together Massed Choirs, hordes of schoolchildren and mammoth brass bands. There were celebrations for the Adoption of the American Constitution, a National Co-operative Day, Home Industrial Exhibition, a Police Fete and a Belgian Day. At all these functions visitors were asked 'to protect the flower beds. There is ample space on the broad gravel walks for tens of thousands of spectators. Please preserve the flowers and turf about from injury.' Visitors were also advised not to pass under or stand near the wires by which the comets (fireworks) descended from the Towers, nor to stroll about the grounds during the displays as the falling rocket sticks could be dangerous.

On 23rd. April 1864 the 300th. Anniversary of the Birth of Shakespeare was commemorated. A full size replica of his house was erected in the centre transept of the Palace and each visitor received a free photograph of the original so that the model might be compared. Photographs and slides featured heavily in the Mammoth Photograph Exhibition of 20th. February 1888, while to prove that there is nothing really new ever invented, Baron Kempelen was on hand to demonstrate his Automaton Chess Player.

The Victorian penchant for self-improvement, or for 'fast' operettas with libretti now long lost to us was given full rein during the Palace's first years. Mr. Ferdinand de Lesseps (of Suez Canal fame) was honoured by a performance of Wallace's 'Maritana', while on Coronation Day in 1870 the glasswork vibrated to Randegger's 'The Rival Beauties'.

Unashamed Improvement came to the fore when the National Temperance League took over in September 1868, with hymn titles on the sheet such as: 'We'll never be drunkards,' 'We love cold water', 'Dash it down' and 'Merry Dick', the first line of which, it must be hastened to add, was 'My Drink is water bright'.

Anyone seeking to escape from all the jousting, displaying and carolling within could seek the Pleasure Grounds, where in September 1882 was to be found 'an electric railway on a new system on the second terrace. The line is 350 yd. in circuit worked by current supplied by a primary dynamo at the foot of the steps leading to the second terrace, the current being transmitted to rails, thence to the dynamo locomotive, to which the cars are electrically connected so as to aid the work of the engine. The speed attained is 18–20mph. The station and booking office are lighted by 37 incandescent lamps and all the signalling is performed by electric current.' If the description from the programme is correct, then this would be an interesting and substantial little line with advanced ideas.

above: The 1882 railway: one of the first in the world

THE PATRICK BEAVER COLLECTION AND THE CRYSTAL PALACE FOUNDATION

below: The 'all red route' at the British Empire Exhibition 1911

ELECTRIC TRAINS IN THE PALACE GROUNDS

Experimental pneumatic railway 1864

CROYDON PUBLIC LIBRARIES
Before the fire – Palace and grounds c 1930

27

A mixed crowd shares the simple pleasures of a fireworks display

6

Halcyon Days

Following the eighties and up to the Great War period the Palace began, slowly, to lose its looks and its hold upon the public, becoming rather tawdry and seedy in its appearance. In many respects it became rather like premises met with nowadays up and down the country, when a large building is taken over and let out into units which are taken up by craft shops, market stalls and bazaar bric a brac.

With the growth of other places of diversion round London, Crystal Palace was really out of fashion by the time that Victoria died. One third of the estate was sold for building, a Receiver was brought in during 1909 to act until 1911 when the City raised nearly one quarter of a million to preserve the Palace for the nation, revitalising it all as a sort of Funland-cum-Motor Museum until 1914. The basic trouble underlying the whole situation was that the building, designed as a temporary structure, had become permanent and presented on the grand scale the same problems as the humble domestic greenhouse, namely the tricky painting of crosspieces, damp and the problem of ageing putty which caused the panes of glass to slip, admitting cold air which in turn nullified the effects of the heating. The new suburbs burgeoning by the Palace now created the means for its ruin, with a myriad household chimneys belching sulphurous fumes into the Sydenham sky to attack the ironwork.

The railways continued to decant their passengers and pick them up again without undue fuss. The major alterations at Low Level had taken place in 1874, and a small signal box and crossover had been put in at Sydenham where the tails of the flying junction rejoined, called Crystal Palace Bank. This cabin on the down side served to split up the block section at busy times and lasted until 1921. There were three cabins working the lines at Low Level, Tunnel at the west end being the most important and open continuously. For safety reasons, the overall roof at Low Level was removed in 1905, as a similar design at Charing Cross had collapsed.

Of all the activities met with at the Palace, possibly the most impressive and successful was the Pageant of Empire which took place in 1911, the year of the Coronation of King George V. For this scaled down models of the

29

various colonial Parliament buildings were erected in the grounds, all linked by a tramway which was called the AllRed Route, which some 3,000 workmen were employed in building. The little line took a further hundred staff to operate, with trains of observation cars running throughout the day at one minute intervals from 10a.m. to 11p.m.. Each train could hold eighty passengers each paying sixpence a time. The journey started below the second terrace, then along parallel with it to Newfoundland and turning south by the Low Level walkway to run past the impressive Canada building with its copy of Big Ben. Next stop India, a circular building, then round a reverse curve and a halt in the open garden next to the Maze. At the lower end of the Park the line passed by Australia through a sheep run, the bush and a vineyard, then over a level crossing into New Zealand through a meat quay and Maori encampment. Here was the final halt, after which the line ran back westwards to its starting point. The sixpenny fare was valid for the round trip from any station, but break of journey meant rebooking. On one day at least ostrich rides were offered as an alternative form of pleasure transport!

The Pageant was due to close on 21st. July, but was extended until September to allow hundreds of thousands to witness 'this living history book of the Rise of London from the days when the Empire City was but a collection of mud flats on the now vanished Fleet.' Yet another extension took closure to the 16th., on which day the ladies who had travelled in daily, paying their own fares to make and repair the costly costumes used in the Pageant, 'wept as they sang "Auld Lang Syne". We have made history by maintaining the Pageant for four months. I should like to charter a fleet of ships and take all my helpers to India with me for the Pageant to be held there'.

EDUCATIONAL "MONSTERS"

7

Electrification on the Grand Scale

In 1903 the London Brighton and South Coast Railway gained authority by an Act to electrify the complete system using AC single phase current conveyed by overhead wire. The area losing ground to the new electric trams, that is between London Bridge and Victoria via Denmark Hill was the first to be converted; work started here in 1906 and the first trial run was made on 17th. January 1909. The Allegemeine Elektricitats Gesselschaft of Berlin were principal contractors and they sub-contracted to British Thomson Houston and Siemens, as well as Blackwell & Co. of Westminster and Johnson & Phillips. Energy was drawn at 6,700 volts AC from the Deptford works of the London Electrical Supply Corporation and supplied to Queens Road Peckham. Six platform lines were electrified at London Bridge and five at Victoria.

To operate the new services eight sets of three bogie vehicles were constructed by the Metropolitan Carriage & Wagon Company of Birmingham. One first class car was set between two motor thirds, giving seats for 74 firsts and 144 thirds. Four 115hp. Winter-Eichberg motors taking 750 volts were fitted to each motor coach. No provision was made for second class travellers in the sets. The original cars were painted in a two tone livery, umber brown lower panels and cream upperworks.

The carriage sheds and works were at Peckham Rye. The public service began on 1st. December 1909 with early steam runs to 7.30 a.m. followed by a fifteen minute headway using the new electrics. The new service promoted as the Elevated Electric was a great success and during the first year of working the number of passengers carried almost doubled. After 1st. June 1912 the entire line was electric, the first class trailer cars were withdrawn and driving trailers were added to the motor coaches which could now run in multiples of one, two or three two-car sets.

The next move was the planning of the line to Crystal Palace Low Level from Battersea Park, continuing through Norwood Junction to the carriage shops and works at Selhurst. The line from Tulse Hill to Peckham Rye was dealt with and also the spurs from Tulse Hill to the Crystal Palace-Norwood line at Leigham Junction and West Norwood Junction.

At the Low Level station three Croydon bays were electrified, and also the up siding at Norwood Junction end of the station. The area around Norwood Junction was also electrified for access to the branch, along with ten roads inside the depot and works at Selhurst. Electric trains conveniently ran from Victoria to Crystal Palace from the west in time for the opening of the Pageant of Empire on 12th. May 1911, carrying a heavy traffic for the four months it was open. The Peckham Rye-Tulse Hill-West Norwood Junction-Leigham Junction line had a delayed opening due to lack of sufficient power available from the generators. However, the electrics ran as from 1st. March 1912 because of a restriction on steam trains due to a Coalminers Strike. Construction was generally the same in principle as with the South London line, except that some of the overhead gear was lighter. The tunnel at Crystal Palace Low Level placed constraints on the new rolling stock, restricting it to 8ft. width. Most of the new stock was built by Metropolitan Cammell Weymann Ltd.; some were refurbished steam motor trailers. Three car sets were provided, with a motor car containing a guard's compartment and seven thirds flanked by two driving trailer composites each with three first and five third class compartments. The motors provided were four 150hp models, and at peak periods two sets could be coupled together. Again, no second class was provided. Total seating was 48 first and 170 third. In all, 30 motor cars and 60 trailers were constructed for the services. The livery was all-over amber with gold lining, while within the firsts were in blue upholstery and thirds in red. Large pictures were provided and enamel advertisements were affixed inside the doors.

The South Eastern and Chatham Railway put on a special steam car service between Beckenham and Crystal Palace Low Level on weekdays for the duration of the Pageant of Empire: with eleven return trips commencing with the 9.42 a.m. from Beckenham Junction, the last departing from Crystal Palace at 11.2 p.m. It continued to run until the withdrawal of passenger services in December 1915.

On Coronation Day itself, 30th. June 1911, the greatest crowds ever including 100,000 children came to the Palace for the Festival of Empire. The Brighton Company ferried 56,000 in 56 special trains, 42 running to Low Level and the rest to Penge on the main line. The SE & CR put on 40, while three off the Midland ran to Sydenham Hill on the main line. Many of the specials were through workings from all parts of the country. The new electric service was suspended, due to congestion.

One of the disadvantages of any steam service must have been its unevenness of departure times. With the onset of electric working came the fixed interval services and, some might say, sheer boredom.

On weekdays from September 1911 there were electric trains from Victoria to Crystal Palace every twenty minutes from 7 to 8 a.m., then a fifteen minute headway to 4 p.m., five trains per hour to 6 p.m. reducing to a fifteen minute

H.C. CASSERLEY

In February 1928 ex LBSC E5 Class no. B404 stands at Low Level with a London Bridge via Forest Hill train. In the background is an overhead electric train and the third rail electrification nears completion

service to 9 p.m. and back to 20 minutes until midnight. From London Bridge trains ran to Crystal Palace on a fifteen minute basis to 11 a.m., then at 20 minute intervals until 11.55 p.m. The trains ran light to and from the depot at Norwood Junction. Passenger revenue in the first months was up by 70%.

The first headcodes were templates with white figures on a black ground. The relevant ones were as follows:
1. Victoria to Crystal Palace.
2. Victoria to Streatham Hill.
3. Victoria to Norwood Junction.
4. London Bridge to Crystal Palace.
5. London Bridge to Victoria.
6. London Bridge to Norwood Junction.

H.J. PATTERSON RUTHERFORD
After completion of the overhead electrification a push & pull train stands in one of the Croydon Bay platforms at Low Level

R.C. RILEY
An electric unit formed of ex LBSC stock augmented with a post war trailer shunts at Crystal Palace East Box in March 1954

34

8

Wartime and Thereafter

By the outbreak of war in 1914 much of the money lost in the Palace venture had been recovered, and things were looking promising. However, as in the case of many other ventures, hostilities put a stop to development and prosperity, and the Palace closed for the duration, being used as a naval barracks. Items of especial value on display were moved to safer quarters. As we noted earlier the FA Cup Final was for many years played at Crystal Palace. Then, as now, football fans on trains were often a menace and if a special were held up on the bank outside Low Level station, then the odds were that it would arrive empty at the platform as the occupants would have alighted and shinned over the fencing into the Park.

Eventually, in 1920 the King reopened the great building which had been revitalised by new funds. Inside, the displays were rather tawdry, though the Imperial War Museum collection was housed there for a time. Outside, the gardens were enlivened by dirt track racing, a dubious environmental asset introduced as a change from the quieter cycling. The statuary was scrubbed and repaired and the weighty eight ton head of Joseph Paxton surveyed the scene as before. What would operate no more were the fountains and water displays, the towers, reservoirs and pumps falling out of use. Inside the concert hall things proceeded as before, except perhaps that there was more brass band music and less of that nebulous Victorian opera. Dame Clara Butt did come to sing and test the stability of the panes of glass, while in April 1923 the delightfully named Miss Carrie Tubb and others gave a rendering of Elgar's 'King Olaf' – (Elgar had had his Empire March turned down for the Pageant of 1911.) In October 1923 a Testimonial Concert was held for Mr. Walter Hedgcock who had started as Organist at the Palace in 1894 and had become its Music Director. The choice of music was still tending towards the obscure, as witness in 1924 when Dvorak's 'The Spectre's Bride' was enacted.

For those of timid disposition needing reassurance of the existence of the prosaic world outside, a footnote to programmes read: 'Passengers for East Croydon and all stations to Coulsdon and Smitham Downs inclusive may leave Crystal Palace Low Level by the 10.15 p.m. train which will be extended to Selhurst. Passengers for Croydon and the Coulsdon line should change at Selhurst.'

The year 1923 saw the merging of the railway companies into four major groups, those south of the Thames being formed into the Southern Railway Company. The Southern inherited the overhead electric system of the Brighton and the simpler 660 volt DC third rail system adopted by the London and South Western Railway. It was committed to a widespread programme of further electrification of the remainder of the suburban network and decided that the South Western's third rail system should become the standard and the Brighton's lines altered to conform. However the Brighton had already embarked on extensions to Sutton and Coulsdon North, and these were converted to overhead working on 1st April 1925. Work on replacement of the overhead by third rail commenced in August 1926 and the first sections altered were from London Bridge to Victoria via the South London line, Streatham Hill and Crystal Palace on 17th. June 1928, while the other Crystal Palace services from Victoria were altered as from 3rd. March 1929. The final train made up of such stock left Victoria for Coulsdon North early on Sunday 22nd. September 1929. For a time afterwards wires were left up from Battersea to Peckham Rye to move rolling stock awaiting disposal. At least one of the heavier overhead wire supports survived long afterwards in use as a cantilever arch for a colour light signal outside Clapham Junction.

The Sydenham-Crystal Palace Low Level-Beckenham Junction section was actually in use with a skeleton service of third rail trains from London Bridge via Forest Hill on 25th. March 1928, until the full service commencing on 17th. June 1928; on the same day new electric signalling was brought in at London Bridge and on that first day certain main line trains were terminated at Crystal Palace Low Level. A new circular service was inaugurated to Crystal Palace travelling out and back to London Bridge half hourly in each direction via Sydenham and Tulse Hill.

Following on the heels of the Victoria to Crystal Palace conversion the third rail was extended to West Croydon and Beckenham Junction. Passenger trains to the latter had ceased on 1st. December 1915 and some fundamental alterations and upgrading had to be done before the new trains could run. Gradients were eased, the mid-Kent line was raised and a new signal box was provided.

Meanwhile the Southern had turned its attention to the former L.C. & D.R. lines. The High Level branch was electrified together with the Victoria to Orpington line and that from Holborn Viaduct to Herne Hill. At Nunhead, where the branch proper diverged from the Catford loop-lines, a new station consisting of a 520ft. island platform was opened on 2nd. May 1925, built west of the old structure. The revitalised lines were fed with 660v.

DC reduced from 11,000v. AC supplied by the London Electrical Supply Company.

Several training runs were made up to High Level from 1st. April 1925, the full public service getting under way on 12th. July 1925. A regular 20 minute interval service was instituted between St. Pauls (now Blackfriars) and Crystal Palace High Level, extended on Saturday afternoons and evenings to Holborn Viaduct. The High Level service was half hourly on Sundays.

CROYDON PUBLIC LIBRARIES
The Palace Towers over the Parade and high level tracks

37

Southern Electric network in South London

9

The Great Conflagration

In the early thirties attendance at the Palace displays and exhibitions had recovered, due largely to the efforts of the administrator Sir Henry Buckland. Visitors would total up to one million each year, bringing in some £80,000 or so. The year 1937 was intended to be an especially good one, particularly with the forthcoming Coronation of Edward VIII, for which one of those splendid gatherings of children had been arranged, 30,000 of them coming to sing with Gracie Fields.

On the night of 30th. November 1936 Sir Henry was on his way home when he noticed a fire in one of the administration offices, a fire which might have been contained if there had not been a strong north west wind blowing. Very soon the conflagration was under way and a firework display beyond even the wildest dreams of Brock could be seen from Brighton as flames rose 300ft. into the air. Eighty-nine fire engines attended the blaze and made their headquarters at the High Level station, the firemen suitably plied with sustenance from the station refreshment rooms. First thoughts must have been to wonder how much glass and iron could cause such an inferno, until one remembers the vast amount of wooden staging, seats and partition work within the building. The glass ran down the terraces before congealing into grotesque cascades, replacing the defunct water displays. A poignant picture shows a crestfallen Sir Henry standing surveying the ruins of his sixteen years of work, which was insured at Lloyd's for a mere £110,000, the organ for £1,000. The two towers and both the stations including the lower walkway were saved, but little else survived apart from the grounds and the prehistoric monsters and statuary. The event made a great impact on the country as a whole, and with hindsight the sensitive saw in the catastrophe an omen of war, much as had been the sinking of the 'Titanic' in 1911. King Edward VIII abdicated ten days after the fire.

A senior employee of the LNER at King's Cross station wrote the following graphic essay on the fire:

'From the Parade, seething with thousands of people, an amazing scene was spread before our wondering eyes. Under the shadow of the vast South tower the huge structure of the South wing was silhouetted against the background of the night sky by the orange flames consuming all within the structure. The glass was pouring from the roof in flaming cascades into the building, setting on fire anything combustible that was not already burning. A group of statuary could be seen against the blaze standing immobile, with flames licking round it until the floor fell with a crash. The intense heat could be felt half a mile away, and firemen in consequence were only able to work for very short periods. The roar of the flames could be heard at even greater distances. A newspaper could be read without difficulty several hundred yards from the blaze. All the time, vast crowds of people were accumulating, and there was not a vantage point unoccupied, faces at every window; trees were swarming with boys; fences and walls all bore their full complement, and rooftops made favourite grandstands. People were approaching on foot, on bicycles, motor cycles, in motor cars, motor buses, trains, trams and trolley buses from all directions. The cry of fire will loosen the most reserved tongue, and many strange stories were heard. People travelled from all over London to see what caused the Oriental sunset which blazed in the southern sky. . . . When the announcement went forth from Broadcasting House that the Crystal Palace was on fire, thousands of people rushed out to obtain the best view, and those who flocked to the vicinity caused the most amazing traffic jam that has ever taken place. So bad was the position on the Parade that it took the police nearly an hour to move the crowd 75 yards. While the multitude was collecting, the fire spread the whole length of the structure; the flue-like formation of the building, aided by a strong north west wind made all efforts to quell the blaze seem futile; in fact, the blaze had assumed such gigantic proportions that the only thing which could be done was to save the north end, which was to windward of the main conflagration, but even so the flames spread surely and slowly against the wind and efforts of the firemen, only the burnt out shell remaining to give mute witness of this ghastly tragedy. The chief cause of anxiety was the South Tower. This tower has always had a slight list, and as it contained much explosive and inflammable material, every effort was made to save it. Had it fallen, who knows, another Fire of London might have started. The tower is situated at the corner of two roads and within 100ft. of the carriageway. The wind would have directed the falling building, had it collapsed, across rows of houses, the occupants of which were evacuated in eventuality of such a catastrophe. The fire brigade's work was greatly hampered by the vast concourse. However, by using prodigious quantities of water on the base of the tower and by blowing up intervening structures which would have spread the conflagration, the two towers still stand mute sentinels over the area of terrible desolation. . . . On this last November night London's transport was faced with a task never before encountered. The steady flow by every manner of locomotion from hub to every point of the suburban perimeter was checked and a reverse stream swiftly formed. Those obtained early knowledge of the whereabouts

R.C. RILEY

31713 & 31576 nearing High Level with empty stock of "Palace Centenarian"
19th Sept 1954

GREATER LONDON COUNCIL

After closure – inside the High Level Station

41

of the calamity spread the tidings and the throng swiftly swelled to incredible proportions. All London's bridges were packed with sightseers. Thus passed an old friend.'

As happened with a similar fire which befell Alexandra Palace when it was first constructed, the place remained a spectacle, a sideshow even in its ruined state, human nature being what it is. Special trains were laid on from High Level to St. Paul's to take many of the sightseers home. The sidings here were used to stable spare stock, steam sets used for special workings such as hop-picking trains, and on the night of the fire two such sets happened to be there, to be used as climbable vantage points for the hundreds of people who wished to get a grandstand view of events. High Level, though quite near to the Palace, came out of things well and settled down to life as a normal suburban station. Low Level suffered more, as the sheer weight of water used above the tunnel at the west end caused a breakdown of the lining which was renewed during the summer of 1937. There was, as a result, single line working between Gipsy Hill and Crystal Palace Tunnel cabin with only Victoria to West Croydon trains running through, other services stopping short at Streatham Hill. A shuttle service was put on between Low Level and Beckenham Junction. Services on the London Bridge circulars terminated at Low Level and Gipsy Hill respectively. It was possible to resume normal working by 3rd. July 1938. During 1937 the Sheffield steel merchant Thomas W. Ward & Co. Ltd. removed 10,000 tons of scrap from the palace site, possibly using that same loading dock at Low Level where all the circus traffic had arrived and from where the occasional fractious elephant had escaped.

SUBWAY FROM HIGH LEVEL TO THE PALACE

10

The Long Hiatus

Thereafter, up to and during the 1939–45 War things were quiet around the Palace site, the two towers, prehistoric monsters and statuary brooding over the past and perhaps curious at the new transmitting aerial which appeared at one corner of the site. It has been said, possibly with truth, that the 85 years of the existence of Crystal Palace were perhaps the most significant in the history of Europe-certainly the aims behind it all were artistic and creative, peaceful in concept and therefore almost too good to survive what was to come in wartime. The towers had to go during the war, the fatuous reason given that they were useful landmarks to the enemy. One likes to consider that our present ways of thinking would have perhaps preserved them, along with the wonderful fountains. Instead there is yet another Temple of Sport embodied in the new National Recreational Centre.

Wartime treated the High Level state as fairly as the fire had done; how the old LC & DR directors would have chuckled over the fortunes of the opposition! There were no direct hits, though anti-aircraft guns shattered much of the glass in the all-over roof. It was never replaced, so that the north end and its rooms were abandoned and left to nesting birds and decay. The tiled subway was used as an air raid shelter.

Low Level lost part of the footbridge connecting the Croydon platforms to the main concourse, while another bomb damaged the north end and caused another bout of single line working for a period. However, services did soldier on at Low Level during the whole of wartime, whereas at High Level there were economies. From 6th. January 1941 trains worked in and out of the station to and from Nunhead, where they connected with the Catford Loop service. The headway was every twenty minutes at peak periods, but half hourly at other times and on Sundays. The branch was totally closed from 1st. May 1944, nicely losing much patronage which was not recovered when the line reopened 3rd. March 1946. The High Level station was used for the storage of rolling stock, with one eminent visitor the 5BEL Pullman unit No. 3052 which was damaged by enemy action in 1940 and not restored until 1947. The intermediate stations on the branch grew more tatty as their patrons dwindled; one station had been bombed, another had suffered a landslide, while the quality of the electric supply feeders left much to be desired. Due to lack of passengers, Sunday services went from 27th. September 1948, and the platforms were used to store spare rolling stock. A

43

H.C. CASSERLEY

Arboreal approach to High Level

single four car electric set was usually found sufficient for most runs to High Level. There was one freight working down the branch from Herne Hill in the early hours, conveying chiefly coal, a working which was transferred to Low Level.

The Crystal Palace grounds had recovered some of their old panache by 1953, after years of neglect, and car racing fixtures attracted considerable crowds. The first of these was held on Whit Monday 1953, bringing 8,000 passengers to Low Level and 1,250 to High Level, the best numbers since the disaster and the last in any quantity. Notwithstanding, the High Level branch closed on 18th. September 1954 and as a panacea extra buses were put on between Honor Oak and Crystal Palace.

At Low Level the Victoria – Beckenham Junction trains had been restored to a twenty minute headway from 7th. October 1946, while the London Bridge-Crystal Palace circulars were increased to the same frequency in rush hours.

The steam workings through Low Level were of great interest, especially those which crossed the river. There was at one time a through service between Willesden Junction and East Croydon via Crystal Palace and Clapham Junction, worked by Webb 2-4-2 tanks and later by 0-6-2 tanks. In 1916, for instance there were five trains each way on weekdays only. After

44

H.J. PATTERSON RUTHERFORD
All quiet at Lordship Lane in the 1920's

H.J. PATTERSON RUTHERFORD
Upper Sydenham in the 1920's

R.C. RILEY

40006 with Willesden Junction to East Croydon vans at Low Level 23rd June
1954

R.C. RILEY

32472 approaches Low Level from the Sydenham Line on "Mid Kent and
West End of London and Crystal Palace Railway Centenary" special 30th
December 1956

Grouping the working was reduced to one service, the 9.14 a.m. ex Willesden arriving at East Croydon at 10.27 and returning at 11.16, something of an oddity as it was not advertised to carry passengers over the Southern section for the reason that being primarily a parcels train schedules could not be guaranteed. Latterly the train became a conditional 9.35 a.m. ex Willesden Junction, back from East Croydon at 11.28 and worked by a Fowler 2-6-2 tank. The inclusion of passenger stock in the formation was discontinued after 14th. September 1940 when the West London Extension line lost its passenger service, due to heavy usage by freight workings which passed through Low Level to and from Willesden or Old Oak Common and Norwood Yard. Usually employed on the freights were Southern 2-6-4 tanks, Midland Region 8F or WD 2-8-0s and occasionally Class 5s. Rarely seen was a Great Western Pannier 0-6-0 tank, while the keen observer could man the platforms in the small hours to catch a small Brighton 0-6-0 or 0-6-2 tank fussily occupied on an Old Oak-Three Bridges freight. Such engines would also work the Low Level pick up goods. The only significant freight workings round to Sydenham were tanker workings between Rotherhithe Road and Clapham Junction.

Accidents and closure of the L, C & D line via Sydenham Hill have occasionally led to unusual workings, as on 30th. June 1954 when no less a train than the down 'Golden Arrow' came through Low Level and on to Beckenham Junction.

To mark the closure of the High Level line an excursion was put on intended to link both the Palaces Alexandra and Crystal, leaving the High Level station on 19th. September with Class C locomotive No. 31576 and assisted by Class D No. 31749 for part of the way. In the event the working did not reach Alexandra Palace but traversed an interesting route via Factory Junction, Richmond, Teddington, Wimbledon, Clapham Junction, back to Factory Junction, Tulse Hill, Low Level, London Bridge, Metropolitan Jc., Elephant & Castle, Nunhead and home again. From Blackfriars engines Nos. 31719 and 31573 were used.

Today the electrics go their well-ordered way albeit less frequently than formerly and just a few rush hour trains on the original line from Sydenham. Low Level is there, suffering from the apparent BR policy of removing bits every so often in the hope that nobody will realise that the place is disappearing. The glass porticos went in 1963, the north mansard roofing in 1976. A working party of locally interested parties was convened to put forward schemes which would bring the station premises into a new project, thus effectively preserving what remains. An indoor sports complex, railway museum and a mini-Crystal Palace were all mooted, but at the time of writing nothing has come of the ideas.

FOOTBALL ASSOCIATION

F.A. Cup Final 1901 Brown scores for Tottenham against Sheffield United

APPENDIX 1

THE CRYSTAL PALACE AND THE EARLY YEARS OF ASSOCIATION FOOTBALL

By the Rev. Nigel Sands MA, Chaplain, Historian and Statistician to Crystal Palace Football Club.

For a period of some twenty years before the 1st World War the Crystal Palace was the great stage for Association Football in England, but the story of this sport at the Palace opens rather earlier, in the 1870's.

A club entitled Crystal Palace Football Club had been formed from the workmen and officials at the Palace at least as early as 1871, and it is known that a representative of it, Mr. D. Allport, was present at the meeting of the Football Association held at the London office of 'The Sportsman' newspaper on July 20th 1871 at which the forming of a Challenge Cup Competition was first discussed. Indeed Mr. Allport was one of the three men charged by the FA in the following year with the responsibility of actually selecting and purchasing the original FA Cup.

The first-ever FA Cup competition was held in 1871-72. Fifteen clubs entered, and, with the aid of the then existing rule under which clubs involved in a drawn game progressed to the next round, the Palace club reached the semi-final. It took part in the first five FA Cup competitions but appears then to have gone out of existence.

Clearly the old Crystal Palace Football Club had a team which did justice to the majestic building. Regrettably there are no records of any of its matches apart from those in the FA Cup from 1872 to 1876, or of any of its teams, but it is known that one of England's forwards in the inaugural international match against Scotland on 30th November 1872, played in a Glasgow fog at Hamilton Crescent, Partick, was one C.J. Chenery of the Palace club. Chenery in fact played in the England front line (the tactics of the period permitted no fewer than seven forwards!) in the first three International clashes, and Crystal Palace also provided the goalkeeper in 1873 (A. Morton) while in 1876 both the goalkeeper (A.H. Savage) and the centre-forward (C.E. Smith) came from the Palace club.

However, the closest association of the Crystal Palace with the FA Cup competition came about in the 20 years from 1895 to 1914 when the Cup Final itself was played at the Palace. The playing enclosure, known sometimes as 'The Exhibition Ground', was adjacent to the Palace itself and to the fairground, and the vast grassy slopes that surrounded it could much better accommodate the growing numbers now wishing to watch the Final than the confined enclosures of Kennington Oval. Indeed, the Surrey County Cricket Club authorities, fearing for their famous pitch on which the finals had been played since the Cup's inception refused to allow it to be used again for major footballing occasions after the 1892 Final there.

Thus, on 20th April 1895, after two Finals in the North, the Palace first played host to the Final tie where Aston Villa met West Bromwich Albion. The gate was recorded at 42,560 and was described in the Sunday Times the following day as a 'monster attendance' and 'a gigantic crowd'. The match itself was won and lost in the opening minute when a shot from Villa's inside-right, Chatt, was diverted by the Albion goalkeeper to John Devey who scored the goal that has gone down in football history as Villa's 'Crystal Palace Thunderbolt'.

In the twenty Finals played at the Crystal Palace between 1895 and 1914 Aston Villa were the most successful club, winning the trophy on each of their four appearances, but Newcastle United actually played in five Finals at the Palace. Poor Newcastle! In spite of only missing two Finals in the seven played between 1905 and 1911 they just could not win at Sydenham. The hoodoo was never broken: in fact it was compounded, first by their 0–1 home defeat in a 5 round in January 1907 by the embryo Crystal Palace club itself, then less than eighteen months old and lying near the foot of the Southern League; and in 1910 when Newcastle actually won the Cup they did so, not at the Palace, but in a replay at Everton!

By 1901 the Crystal Palace Cup Final was capable of drawing an amazing crowd of over 110,000 and there were other six-figure attendances in 1905 and 1913. In fact the gate of 121,919 at the 1913 Final (at which part of a stand roof collapsed under the pressure of those *on top* of it) is the second largest of all time at an English Cup Final and has only ever been exceeded at the famous 'White Horse' Final of 1923, the first final to be played at Wembley.

However, the Crystal Palace played host to other important footballing occasions in addition to the Cup Finals. Chief among these were the England v. Scotland Internationals played there every fourth year from 1897. Among the immortal football personalities to grace this series of four games perhaps the greatest were England's inside-right Steve Bloomer, who played in the 1897, 1901 and 1905 matches and scored in the first two (Bloomer also played in Derby's unsuccessful Cup Final sides of 1898 and 1899), Sam Hardy our goalkeeper from Liverpool, who made his international debut in the 1909 match, and 'Nudger' Needham of Shefleld United who played left-half in the first two clashes and went on to win Cup Winners medals in 1899 and 1902. Vivian Woodward, Alex Leake, Willie-John Sutcliffe, Harold Fleming, Billy (Fatty) Wedlock – they all played for England at the Palace to the delight and appreciation of the football fans of their era.

Such was the interest generated in South East London by these footballing spectaculars that in 1904 the proposal was put to the Football Association that the Crystal Palace Company be permitted to form another football club of its own, but the FA quashed the plan on the grounds that the owners of the Cup Final arena could not promote their own club. However, in 1905 a Crystal Palace Football Club was formed, independent of the Crystal Palace Company but playing on their pitch, and it was elected to the Southern League. It immediately won the 2nd Division Championship and from 1906 was a member of the powerful 1st Division of the Southern League.

The two men most influential in establishing Crystal Palace Football Club were Mr. Edmund Goodman, who was Secretary of it from its foundation and manager from 1907, and the Chairman for 25 years, Mr. Sidney Bourne.

The new club's earliest nickname was 'The Crystals' but they soon became known for obvious reasons as 'The Glaziers'. They were a strong Southern League outfit and came nearest to winning the Championship in 1914 when they were only denied by Swindon Town on goal average.

It was the 1st World War which severed the connection between the Crystal Palace and the football club which bears its name: the Palace itself was requisitioned by the Admiralty, the building and grounds closed to the public from Wednesday 10th February 1915 and Crystal Palace FC played their last match there on Saturday 6th February 1915, beating Reading 4–1. Several fellow Southern League clubs, including neighbours Croydon Common and Millwall, offered their grounds to enable Crystal Palace to complete their fixtures but the Directors decided to make their temporary base at the rather less auspicious surroundings of the Herne Hill running track, and in mid-season, the Palace club left its home.

One brief but attractive chapter remains to be told for in 1922 the famous, all-amateur club, The Corinthians, made the Crystal Palace their headquarters. The Corinthians were of such strength and quality that they were excused the preliminary rounds of the FA Cup competition, their reputation and ability being such that they were always capable of taking the scalp of professional opponents. Thus, again, the Palace arena hosted football of the highest standard, and if the Corinthians 1–0 victory over 1st Division Blackburn Rovers in January 1924 was their best result there are few who will deny that their best performance was in the 1–3 defeat three years later by 1st Division leaders Newcastle United before 56,000 enthralled spectators. The Corinthians led their mighty visitors for nearly an hour; Newcastle only equalised with 15 minutes remaining and the last two goals came in the dying minutes against a depleted and injury-hit Corinthian side.

Relations between the Corinthians and Crystal Palace FC were always cordial and it was fitting that during the inter-war period the two clubs met for friendly, testimonial and charity matches. It was thus during this series of games that the C.P. club returned to its original home – albeit as the visiting side!

APPENDIX 2

TRAMS AND TROLLEYBUSES

The competition between tramway and rail which grew in developing London was less pronounced for the large Crystal Palace traffic than in other areas. Trams came to the Palace only from the south, to the terminus of a branch of the South Metropolitan network which was centred on Croydon.

The line to Crystal Palace Low Level Station from the "Robin Hood" public house on the Croydon Road, Penge was opened on 12th April 1906 but the final section up Anerley Hill was so steep as to require special arrangements. At first two cars were fitted with Spencer track brakes, which could be wound down onto the rails when descending the hill. Later J.S. Rowarth, who was a director of Brush Electrical Engineering and of the B.E.T. which owned South Met, invented a system of regenerative control, by which a car descending a steep hill could use its motors as brakes and generate current which passed back into the overhead wires to be used by other cars ascending. This method of operation had been expected to economise on current consumption but, in practice, the system was 'a guzzler of juice' and after two or three years the special equipment was removed from the cars.

On 26th September 1910 Penge U.D.C. granted the tramway company a building licence for a passenger shelter at the top of Anerley Hill, a small wooden structure on land belonging to the Palace authorities, with a clock visible to tram drivers and with a telephone link direct to the depot; it carried an enamel sign proclaiming: 'S.M.E.T. TRAM SHELTER' (At that period busses were not allowed to use Anerley Hill).

In 1920, ironically, two Metropolitan single deck cars surplus to that company's Alexandra Palace service requirements were transferred and one was used on the Crystal Palace route. This emigration was strongly objected to by the Middlesex County Council whose legend appeared with that of the Metropolitan company on the sides of the cars.

Replacement of the trams by a through service (route 654) of trolley-buses from Crystal Palace to Sutton took place on 9th February 1936 only ten months before the Palace itself was destroyed by fire. Trolley buses continued to operate until replaced by motor bus services on 3rd March 1959.

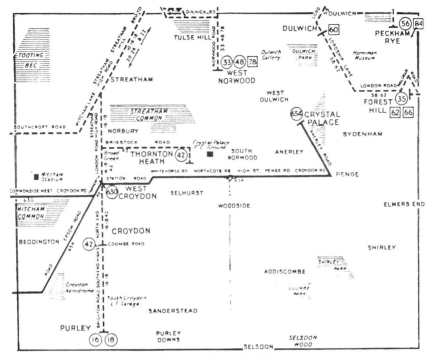

From a Map of 1946

Tram Routes --------- Trolley bus Routes ————

COLLECTION MARTIN CRAVEN

South Metropolitan Car at the Palace

53

LONDON BRIDGE, CRYSTAL PALACE, KENSINGTON, and VICTORIA.—Crystal Palace and West End.

Down. (Column 12 is Saturdays only.)

Mls	Fares 1 cl.	2 cl.	3 cl.	gov	Down.	gov	gov	gov	gov	gov	gov	gov	gov	gov	gov	1,2,3	1,2,3 (Saturdays only)	gov	1,2,3
—					**London Bridge** d	6 25	7 40	8 23	8 47	9 35	1040	1123	1155	1248	1 45	2 12	2 30	2 35	3 10
3	0 8	0 6	0 3	0 3	New Cross	6 32	7 47	8 30	8 54	9 42	1047	1130	12 2	1255	1 52	....	....	2 42	....
—	0 8	0 6	0 3	0 3	Brockley 1	6 36	7 51	8 34	8 58	9 46	1051	1134	12 6	1259	1 56	....	....	2 46	....
5½	1 0	0 8	0 6	0 5½	Forest Hill 2	6 43	7 58	8 41	9 5	9 53	1058	1141	1213	1 6	2 3	....	2 43	2 53	3 23
6½	1 0	0 9	0 6	0 6	Sydenham	6 46	8 1	8 44	9 8	9 56	11 1	1144	1216	1 9	2 6	....	....	2 56	3 26
7½	1 3	1 0	0 7	0 7	**Crystal Palace**	6 52	8 7	8 50	9 12	10 4	11 7	1150	1220	1 15	2 12	2 28	2 48	3 2	3 30
8½	1 3	1 0	0 7	0 7	Gipsy Hill 3	6 55	8 10	8 53	....	10 7	1110	1153	....	1 18	2 15	2 31		3 5	....
9½	1 3	1 0	0 7	0 7	Lower Norwood	6 58	8 13	8 56	....	1010	1113	1156	....	1 21	2 18	2 34		3 8	....
10½	1 3	1 0	0 7	0 7	Streatham Hill	7 2	8 17	9 0	....	1014	1117	12 0	....	1 25	2 22	2 38		3 12	....
10¾	1 3	1 0	0 7	0 7	Balham * [mon	7 5	8 20	9 3	....	1017	1120	12 3	....	1 28	2 25	2 41		3 15	....
13	1 3	1 0	0 7	0 7	Wandswrth Com-	7 8	8 23	9 6	....	1020	1123	12 6	....	1 31	2 28	2 44		3 18	....
13½	1 3	1 0	0 7	0 7	Clapham Junc.	7 12	8 27	9 10	....	1025	1127	1210	....	1 35	2 32	2 48		3 22	....
13¾	1 7	1 3	0 9	0 8	All 1,2,3 class: Battersea	7 53	8 53	9 16	....	1053	1156	1218	....	2 13	....	3 13		3 58	....
15	1 8	1 3	0 9	0 8½	Chelsea	7 56	8 56	9 19	....	1056	1159	1221	....	2 16	....	3 16		4 1	....
15½	1 9	1 4	0 10	0 9	W. Brompton	8 0	9 0	9 23	....	11 0	12 3	1225	....	2 20	....	3 20		4 5	....
16½	1 11	1 6	0 11	0 10	**Kensingtn** ar	8 3	9 3	9 27	....	11 3	12 6	1228	....	2 23	....	3 23		4 8	....
15½	1 3	1 0	0 7	0 7	York Road †	7 17	8 32	....	....	1030	1132	1215	....	1 40	2 38	....		3 27	....
15¾	1 3	1 0	0 7	0 7	Grosvenor Road ‡	7 20	8 35	9 16	....	1033	1135	1218	....	1 43	2 41	2 54		3 30	....
16½	1 3	1 0	0 7	0 7	**Victoria** arr	7 23	8 38	9 19	....	1036	1138	1221	....	1 46	2 44	2 57		3 33	....

Down.	1,2,3	1,2,3	1,2,3	1,2,3	1,2,3	1,2,3	gov	1,2,3	gov	gov	gov	gov	gov
London Bridge d	3 50	4 25	4 50	5 15	5 33	5 53	6 20	7 13	7 48	8 35	9 45	11 0	12 0
New Cross	3 57	....	....	....	5 40	6 0	6 27	7 20	7 55	8 42	9 52	11 7	12 7
Brockley 1	....	....	....	....	....	6 4	6 31	7 24	7 59	8 46	9 56	1111	1211
Forest Hill 2	4 6	4 38	5 3	5 28	5 49	6 11	6 38	7 31	8 6	8 53	10 3	1118	1218
Sydenham	4 9	4 41	5 6	5 31	5 52	6 14	6 41	7 34	8 9	8 56	10 6	1121	1221
Crystal Palace	4 16	4 47	5 12	5 37	5 58	6 20	6 52	7 40	8 15	9 2	1012	1127	1227
Gipsy Hill 3	4 19	4 50	5 15	5 40	6 1	6 23	6 55	7 43	8 18	9 5	1015	1130	1230
Lower Norwood	4 22	4 53	5 18	5 43	6 4	6 26	6 58	7 46	8 21	9 8	1018	1133	1233
Streatham Hill	4 26	4 57	5 22	5 47	6 8	6 30	7 2	7 50	8 25	9 12	1022	1137	1237
Balham * [mon	4 29	5 0	5 25	5 50	6 11	6 33	7 5	7 53	8 28	9 15	1025	1140	1240
Wandswrth Com-	4 32	5 3	5 28	5 53	6 14	....	7 8	....	8 31	9 18	1028	1143	1243
Clapham Junc.	4 36	5 7	5 32	5 57	6 18	6 39	7 12	7 59	8 35	9 22	1032	1147	1247
Battersea	4 48	5 16	5 43	6 13	....	....	7 20	8 18	8 48	9 53	....	....	....
Chelsea	4 51	5 19	5 46	6 16	....	....	7 23	8 21	8 51	9 56	....	....	....
W. Brompton	4 55	5 23	5 50	6 20	6 38	....	7 27	8 25	8 55	10 0	....	....	....
Kensingtn ar	4 58	5 26	5 53	6 23	6 41	....	7 30	8 28	8 58	10 3	....	....	....
York Road †	4 41	5 12	5 37	6 2	6 23	6 44	7 17	8 4	8 40	9 27	1038	1152	1252
Grosvenor Road ‡	4 44	5 15	5 40	6 5	6 26	6 47	7 20	8 7	8 43	9 30	1041	1155	1255
Victoria arr	4 47	5 18	5 43	6 8	6 29	6 51	7 23	8 10	8 46	9 33	1044	1158	1258

Up.

Fares 1 cl.	2 cl.	3 cl.	gov	Up.	gov	1,2,3	1,2,3	1,2,3	1,2,3	1,2,3	1,2,3	1,2,3	gov	gov	1,2,3	gov	gov	gov
				Victoria dep	6 24	7 20	7 50	....	8 12	8 38	8 55	9 28	....	10 8	1030	1153	....	1240
0 4	0 3	0 1	0 1	Grosvenor Road ‡	6 28	....	....	....	....	8 42	....	....	....	1012	....	1157	....	1244
0 4	0 3	0 1	0 1	York Road †	6 30	7 25	....	....	8 17	....	....	....	....	1014	1035	1159	....	1246
0 6	0 4	0 3	0 3	All 1,2,3 class: **Kensingtn** d	6 5	7 15	....	....	....	8 29	8 48	9 12	....	9 56	1015	1148	....	1215
0 6	0 4	0 3	0 3	W. Brompton	6 8	....	....	....	....	8 32	8 51	9 15	....	9 59	1018	1151	....	1218
0 6	0 4	0 3	0 3	Chelsea	6 10	7 19	....	....	....	8 34	8 53	9 17	....	10 1	1020	1153	....	1220
0 6	0 4	0 3	0 3	Battersea	6 13	....	....	....	....	8 37	8 56	9 20	....	10 4	1023	1156	....	1223
0 6	0 4	0 3	0 2½	Clapham Junc.	6 35	7 30	7 58	....	8 22	8 48	9 3	9 36	....	1019	1040	12 4	....	1251
0 9	0 7	0 5	0 4	Wandswrth Com-	6 39	7 34	8 2	....	8 26	8 52	9 7	....	....	1023	....	12 8	....	1255
0 10	0 8	0 6	0 4½	Balham * [mon	6 42	7 37	8 5	....	8 29	8 55	9 10	9 41	....	1026	1045	1211	....	1258
0 10	0 8	0 6	0 6	Streatham Hill	6 46	7 41	8 9	....	8 33	8 59	9 14	9 45	....	1030	1049	1215	....	1 2
1 3	1 0	0 7	0 7	Lower Norwood	6 50	7 45	8 13	....	8 37	9 3	9 18	9 49	....	1034	1053	1219	....	1 6
1 3	1 0	0 7	0 7	Gipsy Hill 3	6 54	7 49	8 17	....	8 41	9 7	9 22	9 53	....	1038	1057	1223	....	1 10
1 3	1 0	0 7	0 7	**Crystal Palace**	6 58	7 53	8 22	8 27	8 45	9 11	9 29	9 57	1018	1043	11 5	1228	1240	1 14
1 3	1 0	0 7	0 7	Sydenham	7 2	7 57	....	8 31	....	....	....	10 1	1022	1047	11 9	1232	1244	1 18
1 3	1 0	0 7	0 7	Forest Hill 2	7 5	8 0	....	8 34	8 50	9 17	....	10 3	1025	1050	1112	1235	1247	1 21
1 3	1 0	0 7	0 7	Brockley 1	7 9	8 4	8 29	....	....	9 21	9 36	....	1029	1054	1116	1239	1251	1 25
1 3	1 0	0 7	0 7	New Cross	7 13	8 8	....	....	....	....	9 40	....	1033	1058	1120	1243	1255	1 29
1 3	1 0	0 7	0 7	**London Bridge** a	7 20	8 15	8 39	8 46	9 2	9 31	9 47	1017	1040	11 6	1127	1250	1 2	1 36

Up.	1,2,3	1,2,3	gov	gov	1,2,3	1,2,3	1,2,3	gov	1,2,3	gov	gov	gov	gov	gov
Victoria dep	1 40	2 25	2 45	3 35	4 11	....	5 9	5 45	6 10	6 53	7 30	8 39	9 40	1119
Grosvenor Road ‡	....	....	2 49	3 39	....	....	....	5 49	....	6 57	7 34	8 43	9 44	1123
York Road †	1 45	....	2 51	3 41	4 16	....	5 14	5 51	6 15	6 59	7 36	8 45	9 46	1125
Kensingtn d	1 25	....	....	2 56	3 40	....	4 53	5 41	6 7	6 12	7 15	8 10	9 22	1042
W. Brompton	1 28	....	....	2 59	3 43	....	4 56	5 44	....	6 15	7 18	8 13	9 25	1045
Chelsea	1 30	....	....	3 1	3 45	....	4 58	5 46	6 11	6 17	7 20	8 15	9 27	1047
Battersea	1 33	....	....	3 4	3 48	....	5 1	5 49	....	6 20	7 23	8 18	9 30	1050
Clapham Junc.	1 50	....	2 56	3 46	4 21	....	5 19	5 56	6 20	7 5	7 41	8 50	9 51	1130
Wandswrth Com-	1 54	....	3 0	3 50	4 25	....	....	6 0	....	7 9	7 45	8 54	9 55	1134
Balham * [mon	....	....	3 3	3 53	4 28	....	5 24	6 3	6 25	7 12	7 48	8 57	9 58	1137
Streatham Hill	1 59	....	3 7	3 57	4 32	....	5 28	6 7	6 29	7 16	7 52	9 1	10 2	1141
Lower Norwood	2 3	....	3 11	4 1	4 36	....	5 32	6 11	6 33	7 20	7 56	9 5	10 6	1145
Gipsy Hill 3	2 7	....	3 15	4 5	4 40	....	5 36	6 15	6 37	7 24	8 0	9 9	1010	1149
Crystal Palace	2 13	2 43	3 19	4 9	4 46	5 5	5 40	6 27	6 41	7 28	8 4	9 13	1014	1153
Sydenham	2 17	2 47	3 23	4 13	4 50	5 9	5 44	6 31	6 45	7 32	8 8	9 17	1018	1157
Forest Hill 2	2 20	2 50	3 26	4 16	4 53	5 12	5 47	6 34	6 48	7 35	8 11	9 20	1021	12 0
Brockley 1	2 24	2 54	3 30	4 20	4 57	5 16	5 51	6 38	6 52	7 39	8 15	9 24	1025	12 4
New Cross	2 28	2 58	3 34	4 24	5 1	5 20	5 55	6 42	6 56	7 43	8 19	9 28	1029	12 8
London Bridge a	2 35	3 5	3 41	4 31	5 8	5 27	6 2	6 49	7 3	7 50	8 26	9 35	1036	1215

Sundays (all 1&2 gov.)

Fares Return			Down.										
			London Bridge dp	8 25	9 40	1 45	2 45	4 45	5 55	7 0	7 50	8 55	10 0
1 0	0 9	0 6	New Cross	8 32	9 47	1 52	2 52	4 52	6 2	7 7	7 57	9 2	10 7
1 0	0 9	0 6	Brockley 1	8 36	9 51	1 56	2 56	4 56	6 6	7 11	8 1	9 6	1011
1 6	1 0	0 9	Forest Hill 2	8 43	9 58	2 3	3 3	5 3	6 13	7 18	8 8	9 13	1018
1 6	1 0	0 10	Sydenham	8 46	10 1	2 6	3 6	5 6	6 16	7 21	8 11	9 16	1021
2 0	1 6	1 0	**Crystal Palace**	8 52	10 7	2 12	3 12	5 12	6 22	7 27	8 17	9 22	1027
2 0	1 6	1 0	Gipsy Hill 3	8 55	1010	2 15	3 15	5 15	6 25	7 30	8 20	9 25	1030
2 0	1 6	1 0	Lower Norwood	8 58	1013	2 18	3 18	5 18	6 28	7 33	8 23	9 28	1033
2 0	1 6	1 0	Streatham Hill	9 3	1018	2 23	3 23	5 23	6 33	7 38	8 28	9 33	1038
2 0	1 6	1 0	Balham * [mon	9 6	1021	2 26	3 26	5 26	6 36	7 41	8 31	9 36	1041
2 0	1 6	1 0	Wandsworth Com-	9 9	1024	2 29	3 29	5 29	6 39	7 44	8 34	9 39	1044
2 0	1 6	1 0	Clapham Junction	9 13	1028	2 33	3 33	5 33	6 43	7 48	8 38	9 43	1048
2 6	1 10	1 2	All 1,2,3 class: Battersea	9 33	1118	3 15	3 58	5 48	7 15	8 13	9 3	10 8	....
2 7	1 11	1 3	Chelsea	9 36	1121	3 18	4 1	5 51	7 18	8 16	9 6	1011	....
2 9	2 0	1 4	West Bromptn	9 40	1125	3 22	4 5	5 55	7 22	8 20	9 10	1015	....
3 0	2 2	1 6	**Kensington** ar	9 43	1128	3 25	4 8	5 58	7 25	8 23	9 13	1018	....
2 0	1 6	1 0	York Road †	9 18	1033	2 38	3 38	5 38	6 48	7 53	8 43	9 48	1053
2 0	1 6	1 0	Grosvenor Road ‡	9 21	1036	2 41	3 41	5 41	6 51	7 56	8 46	9 51	1056
2 0	1 6	1 0	**Victoria** arr	9 24	1039	2 44	3 44	5 44	6 54	7 59	8 49	9 54	1059

Sundays (all 1&2 gov.)

Fares Return			Up.										
			Victoria dep	8 24	9 35	1 30	2 30	3 30	4 30	6 20	7 29	8 40	9 40
0 6	0 4	0 2	Grosvenor Road ‡	8 28	9 39	1 34	2 34	3 34	4 34	6 24	7 33	8 44	9 44
0 6	0 4	0 2	York Road †	8 30	9 41	1 36	2 36	3 36	4 36	6 26	7 35	8 46	9 46
0 9	0 7	0 5	All 1,2,3 class: **Kensington** dp	gov.	9 5	1 2	1 54	2 50	4 23	6 13	7 8	8 35	9 25
0 9	0 7	0 5	West Bromptn		9 8	1 5	1 57	2 53	4 26	6 16	7 11	8 38	9 28
0 9	0 7	0 5	Chelsea		9 11	1 8	2 0	2 56	4 29	6 19	7 14	8 41	9 31
0 9	0 7	0 5	Battersea		9 14	1 11	2 3	2 59	4 32	6 22	7 17	8 44	9 34
0 9	0 7	0 5	Clapham Junction	8 35	9 46	1 41	2 41	3 41	4 41	6 31	7 40	8 51	9 51
1 0	0 9	0 8	Wandsworth Com-	8 39	9 50	1 45	2 45	3 45	4 45	6 35	7 44	8 55	9 55
1 3	1 0	0 10	Balham * [mon	8 42	9 53	1 48	2 48	3 48	4 48	6 38	7 47	8 58	9 58
1 3	1 0	0 10	Streatham Hill	8 46	9 57	1 52	2 52	3 52	4 52	6 42	7 51	9 2	10 2
2 0	1 6	1 0	Lower Norwood	8 50	10 1	1 56	2 56	3 56	4 56	6 46	7 55	9 6	10 6
2 0	1 6	1 0	Gipsy Hill 3	8 55	10 6	2 1	3 1	4 1	5 1	6 51	8 0	9 11	1011
2 0	1 6	1 0	**Crystal Palace**	9 0	1011	2 6	3 6	4 6	5 6	6 56	8 5	9 16	1016
2 0	1 6	1 0	Sydenham	9 4	1015	2 10	3 10	4 10	5 10	7 0	8 9	9 20	1020
2 0	1 6	1 0	Forest Hill 2	9 7	1018	2 13	3 13	4 13	5 13	7 3	8 12	9 23	1023
2 0	1 6	1 0	Brockley 1	9 11	1022	2 17	3 17	4 17	5 17	7 7	8 16	9 27	1027
2 0	1 6	1 0	New Cross	9 15	1026	2 21	3 21	4 21	5 21	7 11	8 20	9 31	1031
2 0	1 6	1 0	**London Bridge** arr	9 23	1034	2 29	3 29	4 29	5 29	7 19	8 28	9 39	1039

1, Station for Upper New Cross and Nunhead; 2, for Lordship Lane; 3, for Upper Norwood. * Balham and Upper Tooting. † York Road and Battersea Park. ‡ Grosvenor Road and Battersea Pier.

For **Additional Trains** between London Bridge & Kensington and Victoria, *via* Thornton Heath, see page 66; between Crystal Palace and Victoria and Kensington, see pages 66 and 67.

From 1876 Bradshaw

SOUTH LONDON LINE.—London, Brighton, and South Coast.

☞ **For other Trains** between London Bridge and Peckham Rye, see pages 62 and 63.

Week Days.—*Continued below.*

Down.	a	a	a																													
London Bridge....dep	5 0	5 45	6 15	6 35	7 0	7 23	7 35	7 50	8 10	8 30	....	9 5	9 18	9 35	9 50	10 5	1020	1035	1050	11 5	1120	1142	1150	12 5	1220	1235	1250	1 5	1 20	1 35	1 50	2 5
South Bermondsey....	5 5	5 50	6 20	6 40	7 5	7 28	7 40	7 55	8 15	....	8 50	9 10	9 23	9 40	9 55	1010	1025	1040	1055	1110	1125	1147	1155	12 9	1225	1240	1255	1 10	....	1 40	....	2 10
Old Kent Rd.&Hatcham	5 9	5 54	6 24	6 44	7 9	7 32	7 44	7 59	8 19	8 37	8 54	9 14	....	9 44	9 59	1014	1029	1044	1059	1114	1129	1151	1159	1211	1229	1244	1259	1 14	1 26	1 44	....	2 14
Queen's Road, Peckham	5 11	5 56	6 26	6 46	7 11	7 34	7 46	8 1	8 21	8 39	8 56	9 16	....	9 46	10 1	1016	1031	1046	11 1	1116	1131	1153	12 1	1214	1231	1246	1 1	1 16	1 28	1 46	1 57	2 16
Peckham Rye.........	5 14	5 59	6 29	6 49	7 14	7 37	7 49	8 4	8 24	8 42	8 59	9 19	9 28	9 49	10 4	1019	1034	1049	11 4	1119	1134	1156	12 4	1217	1234	1249	1 4	1 19	1 31	1 49	2 0	2 19
Denmark Hill.....[ton	5 17	6 2	6 32	6 52	7 17	7 40	7 52	8 7	8 27	8 46	9 2	9 22	9 31	9 52	10 7	1022	1037	1052	11 7	1122	1137	1159	12 7	1220	1237	1252	1 7	1 22	1 34	1 52	2 3	2 22
Loughbro' Park & Brix-	5 21	6 6	6 36	6 56	7 21	7 44	7 56	8 11	8 31	8 51	9 6	9 26	9 35	9 56	1011	1026	1041	1056	1111	1126	1141	12 3	1211	1224	1241	1256	1 11	1 26	1 38	1 56	2 7	2 26
Clapham & N.Stockwell	5 25	6 10	6 40	7 0	7 25	7 48	8 0	8 15	8 35	8 55	9 10	9 30	9 39	10 0	1015	1030	1045	11 0	1115	1130	1145	12 7	1215	1228	1245	1 0	1 15	1 30	1 42	2 0	2 11	2 30
Wandsworth Road.....	5 27	6 12	6 42	7 2	7 27	7 50	8 2	8 17	8 37	8 57	9 12	9 32	9 41	10 2	1017	1032	1047	11 2	1117	1132	1147	12 9	1217	1230	1247	1 2	1 17	1 32	1 44	2 2	2 13	2 32
York Rd.&BatterseaPrk	5 30	6 15	6 45	7 5	7 30	7 53	8 5	8 20	8 40	9 0	9 15	9 38	9 43	10 5	1019	1038	1049	11 5	1119	1135	1149	1212	1219	1236	1249	1 5	1 19	1 37	1 46	2 5	2 15	2 35
Grosvenor Road ¶.....	5 33	6 18	6 48	7 8	7 33	7 56	8 8	8 23	8 43	9 3	9 18	9 41	....	10 8	....	1041	....	11 8	....	1138	....	1215	....	1239	....	....	....	1 40	....	2 8	....	2 38
Victoria...........arr	5 36	6 21	6 51	7 11	7 36	7 59	8 11	8 26	8 46	9 6	9 21	9 44	....	1011	....	1044	....	1111	....	1141	....	1218	....	1242	....	....	....	1 43	....	2 11	....	2 41

Week Days—*Continued.*

Down—*Continued.*																																
London Bridge....dep	2 20	2 35	2 50	3 5	3 20	3 35	3 50	4 3	4 20	4 37	4 50	5 3	5 24	5 35	5 48	6 6	6 20	6 40	6 50	7 5	7 20	7 38	7 50	8 5	8 30	9 5	9 35	10 5	1035	11 5	1135	1215
South Bermondsey....	....	2 40	2 55	3 10	3 25	3 40	....	4 8	4 25	4 42	....	5 8	5 29	5 40	5 53	6 11	6 25	6 45	6 55	7 10	7 25	7 43	7 55	8 10	8 35	9 10	9 40	1010	1040	1110	1140	1220
Old Kent Rd.&Hatcham	....	2 44	2 59	3 14	3 29	3 44	3 56	4 12	4 29	4 46	4 56	5 12	5 33	5 44	5 57	6 15	6 29	6 49	6 59	7 14	7 29	7 47	7 59	8 14	8 39	9 14	9 44	1014	1044	1114	1144	1224
Queen's Road, Peckham	2 27	2 46	3 1	3 16	3 31	3 46	3 58	4 14	4 31	4 48	4 58	5 14	5 35	5 46	5 59	6 17	6 31	6 51	7 1	7 16	7 31	7 49	8 1	8 16	8 41	9 16	9 46	1016	1046	1116	1146	1226
Peckham Rye.........	2 30	2 49	3 4	3 19	3 34	3 49	4 1	4 17	4 34	4 51	5 1	5 17	5 38	5 49	6 2	6 20	6 34	6 54	7 4	7 19	7 34	7 52	8 4	8 19	8 44	9 19	9 49	1019	1049	1119	1149	1229
Denmark Hill.....[ton	2 33	2 52	3 7	3 22	3 37	3 52	4 4	4 20	4 37	4 54	5 4	5 20	5 41	5 52	6 5	6 23	6 37	6 57	7 7	7 22	7 37	7 55	8 7	8 22	8 47	9 22	9 52	1022	1052	1122	1151	1232
Loughbro' Park & Brix-	2 37	2 56	3 11	3 26	3 41	3 56	4 8	4 24	4 41	4 58	5 8	5 24	5 45	5 56	6 9	6 27	6 41	7 1	7 11	7 26	7 41	7 59	8 11	8 26	8 51	9 26	9 56	1026	1056	1126	1156	1235
Clapham & N.Stockwell	2 41	3 0	3 15	3 30	3 45	4 0	4 12	4 28	4 45	5 2	5 12	5 28	5 49	6 0	6 13	6 31	6 45	7 5	7 15	7 30	7 45	8 3	8 15	8 30	8 55	9 30	10 0	1030	11 0	1130	12 0	....
Wandsworth Road.....	2 43	3 2	3 17	3 32	3 47	4 2	4 14	4 30	4 47	5 4	5 14	5 30	5 51	6 2	6 15	6 33	6 47	7 7	7 17	7 32	7 47	8 5	8 17	8 32	8 57	9 32	10 2	1032	11 2	1132	12 2	....
York Rd.&BatterseaPrk	2 45	3 5	3 19	3 36	3 49	4 5	4 16	4 33	4 49	5 7	5 16	5 33	5 53	6 5	6 17	6 37	6 49	7 12	7 19	7 35	7 51	8 10	8 20	8 37	9 0	9 37	10 5	1035	11 5	1136	12 7	....
Grosvenor Road ¶.....	....	3 8	....	3 39	....	4 8	....	4 36	....	5 10	....	5 36	....	6 8	....	6 40	....	7 15	....	7 38	7 54	8 13	8 23	8 40	9 3	9 40	10 8	1038	11 8	1139	1210	....
Victoria...........arr	....	3 11	....	3 42	....	4 11	....	4 39	....	5 13	....	5 39	....	6 11	....	6 43	....	7 18	....	7 41	7 57	8 16	8 26	8 43	9 6	9 43	1011	1041	1111	1142	1213	....

SUNDAYS.—London Bridge to Victoria at 8, 8½, 9, 9½, 10, and 10½ mrn.; 1, 1½, 2, 2½, 3, 3 32, 4, 4½, 5, 5½, 6, 6½, 7, 7½, 7 57, 8 33, 9 3, 9½, 10, 10½, and 11 5 aft., calling at all Stations at same intervals as on Week Days.

Week Days.—*Continued below.*

Up.																																	
Victoria...........dep		6 30	....	6 50	7 5	7 23	....	7 43	....	8 5	8 15	8 20	8 33	8 42	....	9 5	9 21	9 37	....	10 2	....	1035	....	11 5	....	1130	....	12 5	....	1235	....	1 5	....
Grosvenor Road ¶.....		6 34	....	6 54	7 9	7 27	....	7 47	....	8 9	8 19	8 24	....	8 46	....	9 9	9 25	....	....	10 6	....	1039	....	11 9	....	1134	....	12 9	....	1239	....	1 9	....
York Rd.&BatterseaPrk		6 36	....	6 56	7 11	7 29	....	7 49	....	8 11	8 21	8 31	8 41	8 51	....	9 11	9 29	9 41	9 56	1011	1026	1041	1056	1111	1126	1139	1156	1211	1226	1241	1256	1 11	1 26
Wandsworth Road.....		6 39	....	6 59	7 14	7 32	....	7 52	....	8 14	8 24	8 34	8 44	8 54	....	9 14	9 32	9 44	9 59	1014	1029	1044	1059	1114	1129	1142	1159	1214	1229	1244	1259	1 14	1 29
Clphm & N.Stokwll a		6 41	....	7 1	7 16	7 34	....	7 54	....	8 16	8 26	8 36	8 46	8 56	....	9 16	9 34	9 46	10 1	1016	1031	1046	11 1	1116	1131	1144	12 1	1216	1231	1246	1 1	1 16	1 31
Loughbro'P.&Brix-	5 0	6 45	6 55	7 5	7 20	7 38	7 48	7 58	8 10	8 20	8 30	8 40	8 50	9 0	9 10	9 20	9 38	9 50	10 5	1020	1035	1050	11 5	1120	1135	1148	12 5	1220	1235	1250	1 5	1 20	1 35
Denmark Hill [ton	5 3	6 48	6 58	7 8	7 23	7 41	7 51	8 1	8 13	8 23	8 33	8 43	8 53	9 3	9 13	9 23	9 41	9 53	10 8	1023	1038	1053	11 8	1123	1138	1151	12 8	1223	1238	1253	1 8	1 23	1 38
Peckham Rye....	5 7	6 52	7 2	7 12	7 27	7 45	7 55	8 5	8 17	8 27	8 37	8 47	8 57	9 7	9 17	9 27	9 45	9 57	1012	1027	1042	1057	1112	1127	1142	1155	1212	1227	1242	1257	1 12	1 27	1 42
Queen's R., Peckhm	5 10	6 55	7 5	7 15	7 30	7 48	7 58	8 8	8 20	8 30	8 40	8 50	9 0	9 10	9 20	9 30	9 48	10 0	1015	1030	1045	11 0	1115	1130	1145	1158	1215	1230	1245	1 0	1 15	1 30	1 45
OldKentR&Htchm	5 12	6 57	7 7	7 17	7 32	7 50	8 0	8 10	8 22	8 32	8 42	8 52	9 2	9 12	9 22	9 32	9 50	10 2	1017	1032	1047	11 2	1117	1132	1147	12 0	1217	1232	1247	1 2	1 17	1 32	1 47
South Bermondsey	5 15	7 0	7 10	7 20	7 35	7 53	8 3	8 13	8 25	8 35	8 45	8 55	9 5	9 15	9 25	9 35	9 53	10 5	1020	1035	1050	11 5	1120	1135	1150	12 3	1220	1235	1250	1 5	1 20	1 35	1 50
London Bridge arr	5 20	7 5	7 15	7 25	7 40	7 58	8 8	8 18	8 30	8 40	8 50	9 0	9 10	9 20	9 30	9 40	9 58	1010	1025	1040	1055	1110	1125	1140	1155	12 8	1225	1240	1255	1 10	1 25	1 40	1 55

Week Days—*Continued.*

Up—*Continued.*																																
Victoria...........dep	....	....	2 5	....	2 32	....	3 4	....	3 38	....	4 8	....	4 36	....	5 6	....	5 25	....	6 5	....	6 26	....	7 7	....	7 45	8 19	8 50	9 19	9 45	1015	1050	1130
Grosvenor Road ¶.....	....	....	2 9	....	2 36	....	3 8	....	3 42	....	....	....	4 40	....	....	....	....	....	6 9	....	6 40	....	....	....	7 49	8 23	8 54	9 28	9 49	1019	1054	1134
York Rd.&BatterseaPrk	1 41	1 56	2 11	2 26	2 38	2 56	3 11	3 26	3 44	3 56	4 15	4 26	4 42	5 0	5 12	5 26	5 33	5 58	6 11	6 26	6 42	6 56	7 13	7 26	7 51	8 26	8 56	9 26	9 51	1021	1056	1136
Wandsworth Road.....	1 44	1 59	2 14	2 29	2 41	2 59	3 14	3 29	3 47	3 59	4 18	4 29	4 45	5 3	5 15	5 29	5 37	6 1	6 14	6 29	6 45	6 59	7 16	7 29	7 54	8 29	8 59	9 29	9 54	1024	1059	1139
Clapham & N.Stockwell	1 46	2 1	2 16	2 31	2 43	3 1	3 16	3 31	3 49	4 1	4 20	4 31	4 47	5 5	5 17	5 31	5 40	6 3	6 16	6 31	6 47	7 1	7 18	7 31	7 56	8 31	9 1	9 31	9 56	1026	11 1	1141
Loughbro' Park & Brix-	1 50	2 5	2 20	2 35	2 47	3 5	3 20	3 35	3 53	4 5	4 24	4 35	4 51	5 9	5 21	5 35	5 45	6 7	6 20	6 35	6 51	7 5	7 22	7 35	8 0	8 35	9 5	9 35	10 0	1030	11 5	1145
Denmark Hill.....[ton	1 53	2 8	2 23	2 38	2 50	3 8	3 23	3 38	3 56	4 8	4 27	4 38	4 54	5 12	5 24	5 38	5 49	6 10	6 23	6 38	6 54	7 8	7 25	7 38	8 3	8 38	9 8	9 38	10 3	1033	11 8	1148
Peckham Rye.........	1 57	2 12	2 27	2 42	2 54	3 12	3 27	3 42	4 0	4 12	4 31	4 42	4 58	5 16	5 28	5 42	5 54	6 14	6 27	6 42	6 58	7 12	7 29	7 42	8 7	8 42	9 12	9 42	10 7	1037	1112	1152
Queen's Road, Peckham	2 0	2 15	2 30	2 45	2 57	3 15	3 30	3 45	4 3	4 15	4 34	4 45	5 1	5 19	5 31	5 45	5 57	6 17	6 30	6 45	7 1	7 15	7 32	7 45	8 10	8 45	9 15	9 45	1010	1040	1115	1155
Old Kent Rd.&Hatcham	2 2	2 17	2 32	2 47	2 59	3 17	3 32	3 47	4 5	4 17	4 36	4 47	5 3	5 21	5 33	5 47	5 59	6 19	6 32	6 47	7 3	7 17	7 34	7 47	8 12	8 47	9 17	9 47	1012	1042	1117	1157
South Bermondsey....	2 5	2 20	2 35	2 50	3 2	3 20	3 35	3 50	4 8	4 20	4 39	4 50	5 6	5 24	5 36	5 50	6 2	6 22	6 35	6 50	7 6	7 20	7 37	7 50	8 15	8 50	9 20	9 50	1015	1045	1120	12 0
London Bridge....arr	2 10	2 25	2 40	2 55	3 7	3 25	3 40	3 55	4 13	4 25	4 44	4 55	5 11	5 29	5 41	5 55	6 7	6 27	6 40	6 55	7 11	7 25	7 42	7 55	8 20	8 55	9 25	9 55	1020	1050	1125	12 5

WORKMEN'S TRAINS.—Victoria to London Bridge at 5, 5½, and 6 mrn.; Loughbro' Park to London Bridge at 5¼, 5¾, 6 5, and 6½ mrn., calling at all Stations.
SUNDAYS.—**Victoria to London Bridge** at 7¾, 8¼, 8¾, 9¼, 9¾, 10 20, and 10 48 mrn.: 1¼, 1¾, 2¼, 2¾, 3¼, 3¾, 4¼, 4¾, 5¼, 5¾, 6¼, 6¾, 7¼, 7¾, 8¼, 8 44, 9 14, 9¾, 10 14, and 10 44 aft., calling at all Stations at same intervals as on Week Days.

a Workmen's Cheap Trains. ¶ Grosvenor Road and Battersea Pier.

From 1876 Bradshaw

THE CRYSTAL PALACE FOUNDATION

Aware that the Crystal Palace site had languished for far too long, the Crystal Palace Foundation, a charitable voluntary organization was formed in 1979 by a small group of local residents interested in the Palace's history and who earlier that year staged a one day exhibition at the National Sports Centre.

The Foundation soon began promoting the memory of the Palace and to enhance the public amenities of the site as well as initially undertaking the partial restoration of the Victorian terraces. In addition, the Foundation has been instrumental in responding to the overwhelming demand for Crystal Palace information, by organizing well attended events, talks, exhibitions, guided tours of the Palace site, oral history interviews and publications – as well as providing schools and other organizations with educational presentations.

Today the Foundation has emerged as the leading authority on the Crystal Palace history and in 1988 established the Crystal Palace Museum which has been created within the former part of the Palace's school of engineering and is the only original building within the Palace grounds to survive the fire of 1936.

Visitors to the museum are greeted by the huge mural depicting the interior of the Crystal Palace, with the inside of the museum decorated with greenery, statues and flags of all nations to recreate the atmosphere of the old Palace.

In addition to various historical Palace items on display including models, Victorian porcelain, books and paintings, the museum also holds an original John Logie Baird 'Televisor' which had been produced at the Palace in 1930. The museum also features video film of the Palace and music that once could be heard at the Crystal Palace.

At present the museum, which is located on Anerley Hill is open Sundays and Bank holidays (11am-5pm) – admission is free. Souvenirs and other publications on the Palace are all available from the museum shop. For further details of the Museum or the Foundation contact the CPF at 84 Anerley Road, London, SE19 2AH (Telephone 081-778 2173)

Members are entitled to many benefits of the Foundation plus free regular issues of the Foundation's own Magazine 'New Crystal Palace Matters' which is full of CPF News, Members' letters, diary of forthcoming events and interesting articles on the Crystal Palace.

If you are interested in joining the Foundation Membership application forms are available from the museum, at any CPF event or upon request from the above address.

Registered Charity N° 285563